NEW RETAIL: BORN IN CHINA GOING GLOBAL

HOW CHINESE TECH GIANTS ARE CHANGING GLOBAL COMMERCE

Rave Reviews

"If, like me, you constantly wonder what the future of retail looks like then "New Retail: Born In China Going Global" will help uncover the answers. Virtually all the real innovation in retail is currently happening in China and Ashley and Michael provide the reader with an informed and expert guide to what the future might hold for all of us."

— **Andrew Busby, Founder and CEO, Retail Reflections, Forbes contributor, Global Top 20 Retail Influencer, IBM Futurist**

"While many believe Amazon leads the world in retail innovation, the truth is China's retail leaders such as Alibaba, Tencent and others are paving a revolutionary path with mobile payments, retail and customer experiences. Ashley and Michael give us an in depth look at China's New Retail revolution."

— **Bryan Eisenberg, New York Times Best Selling Author, co-author of Be Like Amazon: Even a Lemonade Stand Can Do It**

"This wonderfully written and insightful book is, as you would expect from these proven authors, a revelation showcasing that the future is now significantly predicated on the ambitions and appetites of the Asian superpowers of retail and none is more willing to challenge the frontiers than mainland China. Highly recommended for those who enjoy leading into the future. Thank you Ashley and Michael."

— **Brian Walker, Founder, Retail Doctor Group, Vend Top 50 Global Retail Influencers 2018/19, LinkedIn Top Global Retail Voice 2018**

"Ashley Dudarenok and Michael Zakkour portray how in China, it's not about a retail apocalypse but a retail renaissance. With a large number of interesting examples and cases, the authors bring to light how the retail landscape is evolving in China, which should provide plenty of insights and impetus for anyone dealing with retail around the world. Dudarenok and Zakkour write with a clear and easy style and provide a great inside look at the world of retail in China."

— **Minter Dial, speaker, award-winning filmmaker and author of Futureproof and Heartificial Empathy**

"The gravitational force of retail has moved east and industry executives that ignore this monumental shift do so at their peril. "New Retail" is a concise, no-nonsense look into one of the most profound revolutions in retail history. Authors Michael Zakkour and Ashley Galina Dudarenok provide a clear and well-documented narrative on how companies like Alibaba, JD and Tencent are, quite literally, reinventing the modern concept of retail."

— **Doug Stephens, Founder of Retail Prophet and Author of Reengineering Retail: The Future of Selling in a Post-Digital World**

"Amazon often gets all the glory, but the big tech giants of China are the real trailblazers when it comes to digital innovation. Dudarenok and Zakkour expertly dissect the strategies of China's leading retailers, the evolving Chinese consumer, and the technologies that will redefine brick and mortar stores to enable a genuinely frictionless customer experience. The future of retail is already happening in China; this book will give Western retailers a glimpse of what's coming next."

— **Natalie Berg, Retail Analyst, Author and Founder, NBK Retail**

"I've been personally writing for some time that China is the digital laboratory for the future of retail. This is now confirmed in the new book "New Retail: Born In China Going Global" by Ashley Galina Dudarenok and Michael Zakkour. Alibaba, JD, and Tencent are forever changing the global retail delivery model and the lessons from the East will soon reach the West. This book is required reading for its multiple disruptive innovation examples that are foundational to the inevitable digital transformation of the retail delivery model."

— **Tony D'Onofrio, CEO of TD Insights and Top 100 Global Retail Influencer/ Futurist**

"With AI and digital technologies, New Retail redefines e-commerce. It's a retail ecosystem that blends online and offline channels to feature the consumer at the center, often in new and unexpected ways. This timely book is a must-have reference for multinationals to rethink their marketing strategy in China."

— **Winston Ma, former Managing Director of China Investment Corporation (CIC), author of China's Mobile Economy and Digital Silk Road**

To all those people, brands and retailers looking for a greater understanding of China and the future of commerce. This book is for you.

Ashley Galina Dudarenok

To my friends and family for their love and for tolerating the madness and neuroses that go along with writing a book.
In loving memory of my grandparents.

Michael Zakkour

If you want to see the future of retail, you don't need a time machine or a multi-million dollar research initiative. You just need airfare to Shanghai and a week to explore.

CONTENTS

PART III

The New Retail Live: What's Ahead

Introduction

We'd like to take a moment to reflect and share our thoughts on the book's title. We claim that New Retail was born in China and is now going global and we claim that the tech titans of Asia are changing commerce. Let's explain our thinking.

The term New Retail was coined by Alibaba chairman Jack Ma in 2016 to express how he, CEO Daniel Zhang and his team would build the Alibaba Group ecosystem by integrating online and offline, thereby expanding ways of living, communicating, sharing, building, teaching, consuming and "making it easy to do business anywhere."

That said, all of the elements that make up New Retail weren't born or invented in China, or by Alibaba, JD, Tencent, Kaola, Pinduoduo or Xiaohongxu. New technologies, new retail concepts, innovations in e-commerce, fulfillment, logistics, and media, store formats, digital marketing and consumer journey plotting were simultaneously being developed in the United States, Europe, Asia and other parts of the world.

Amazon and the "Amazon Effect" disrupted the very concept of what e-commerce is and could be, trampled the conventional wisdom about what makes for good retail and shopping in the US and changed the value streams, margins and economics of selling products online and off.

Amazon has spent twenty years building a massive ecosystem of products, services, companies, logistics structures and technologies, many of which were and are precursors and foundations for New Retail. If the only thing they had done was Amazon Prime, the game changer in fulfillment, their contribution to New Retail would still be massive.

Digital native and direct to consumer brands were born in the US and over the last several years have disrupted the businesses of traditional consumer packaged goods companies, premium brands and the very idea that manufacturers and brands had to operate on a B2B model in order to get in front of consumers and sell at scale. These companies proved that you could make a great product, create a strong brand, put it online, bypassing wholesale to retail sales and brick and mortar stores, and still provide consumers with a superior experience, lower prices and less transactional friction. Many of these brands are now opening brick and mortar locations. Brick and mortar going digital and digital-only going brick and mortar is one of the signature hallmarks of New Retail.

Apple pioneered the concept of a brick and mortar location being an experience, not a solely a venue for transactions. With the Genius Bar, the brilliant architecture, the vibe of the place and the specific demographics it wanted to draw in, it was all brilliant.

Germany's Rocket Internet not only showed that they could build internet-first brands, they proved that they could build marketplaces for entire regions. When Rocket built and launched Lazada for Southeast Asia it was a milestone in the development of global retail. Japan's Rakuten and their incredible mix of services, internet marketplaces, loyalty and points programs and games was a pioneer in mixing commerce with services and entertainment.

We could document many more significant innovations, contributors and brilliant thinkers who have blazed the trail from digital commerce to New Retail and contributed to the evolution of modern commerce, but that prequel will have to wait.

So what happened in China that led to New Retail being born there. Alibaba was the first company to define and aggressively move forward with "the complete integration of online, offline, technology and logistics" and the first to take all of the assets of their ecosystem - digital payments, logistics, B2C, B2B, D2C, B2B2C, cloud computing, data science, a marketing arm, and brick and mortar - and blend them to create a new model of how to make, move, sell, buy and deliver products.

JD.com, Tencent and others quickly followed quickly in establishing their own ecosystems and integrated all of the needed assets and components.

What also marked the evolution of New Retail was the immediate recognition in China of the importance of physical footprints and experiences. There was a rapid digitization of the physical and a transition from the omnichannel model and the tech titans of China were able to move rapidly and smartly to build an entirely new way of conducting commerce.

What about going global? We're in the early stages of seeing the mature, China/APAC version of New Retail being deployed globally, but it's happening. We're seeing it manifest in the following ways:

- Global brands and retailers who have been doing business in China and are engaged in New Retail are taking what they are doing and learning in Asia and bringing it back to their home markets, and other markets.

- Major global e-commerce titans are building out mega-ecosystems and integrated habitats.

- Major global retailers are adopting New Retail models, technologies and integration to build their own ecosystems and habitats.

- Individual brands are adopting ideas, models, technologies and integration for themselves.

In the following pages we will dive into the topic but this book is not a "how to" guide. It doesn't provide "10 Easy Steps to New Retail Nirvana" and it doesn't provide a panacea for what ails you. Every brand, every retailer, every category and every product is different and requires a different strategy, structure, and implementation for New Retail.

We give context, details and explain the nature of New Retail. There are case studies, some top level advice and, most importantly, information to empower you to take action.

PART I

What is New Retail?

CHAPTER 1

40 Years of Reform

It might be the transformation of the Pudong area of Shanghai from farmland to futuristic mega-city. It might be the metamorphosis of Shenzhen from fishing village to urban tech hub. Perhaps it's the emergence of China as the world's second largest economy or the rise of hundreds of millions to middle-class living standards.

The question we're trying to answer is, "What best symbolizes China's re-emergence as a prosperous world power?"

The answer is, all of the above and so much more.

We don't think there's anyone inside or outside of China who foresaw the size, scale, depth and breadth of China's transformation in less than half a century.

The story of China's development over the last forty years is one of the most fascinating stories in modern history. "Reform and Opening Up" wasn't the result of a single decision, person, meeting or plan. It wasn't a single event launched at a definable moment with a linear series of predictable outcomes. Rather, it was a story of necessity, debate, compromise, experimentation, adjustments, false starts, detours, successes and long-term commitments by the government and the people which have led to a transformation in the lives of 20% of humanity.

Having said that, it's important to note that some of the greatest success stories of the "New China" era have also created challenges that still need to be overcome. These include: how China takes a positive and active role in the global community, how it addresses pollution and sustainability, how it deals with key resources and the transition to a consumption, services and innovation led economy.

Change

It's been said that insanity is "doing the same thing over and over and expecting a different result" and it can be argued that China's modern reform era was born of this realization. After the struggles and wars of the first half of the 20th century that led to the founding of the People's Republic of China in 1949, the country embarked on a program of modernization and nation-building.

There were some notable achievements and a number of prominent setbacks between 1949 and 1979, but it had become clear that China could not meet the needs of its people, in terms of modernization, economic growth and advancement, without changing the approach to it's economy and its relations with the outside world

An incremental and wide reaching set of reforms were introduced between 1980 and 2010 whose most important outcomes were that hundreds of millions were lifted out of poverty, China rejoined the global economic, cultural and political community and the vast majority of Chinese people now enjoy a higher standard of living, economic security and modernity that was previously unimaginable. The alleviation of human want in China is the true starting point for the rest of our story.

A Re-emergence

In 1949, China started anew after a long period of war and upheaval as a newly whole, newly independent and newly confident power, though it would take time to fully re-establish itself on the world stage.

It's often said in the West that China has "emerged" as a world power, economic growth engine, cultural force and military giant over the last 40 years. The truth is that China has re-emerged into these positions. China was in many important ways out-developed and outperformed by the West during the 18th to 20th centuries. But even so, China maintained a grip on economic, trade, scientific and cultural power through the 19th century.

China, during the last 100 years, first established a "new China" followed by a "new, new China", and this has required a focus on internal development.

Reform and Opening Up was the late 20th and early 21st century vehicle that enabled China to start focusing on and building its connection to and position in the external world. At the end of these forty years, China has re-emerged into many of the positions it held for the better part of 2,000 years.

Technology

Over the last forty years, technology has evolved from something that enabled science, engineering, business and productivity, to a ubiquitous part of everyday life. A key achievement in China's modern history is the deliberate and focused development of the country as a global producer of new technologies and new innovations in digital commerce.

China has taken its place alongside the United States as a major creator, driver and user of technology for commercial use.

Tencent's WeChat has become an operating system for people's daily lives, while Alibaba, JD, Kaola, Baidu, Netease and other tech giants are redefining almost every aspect of daily life. Tech savvy Chinese consumers power the consumer economy and have become vital to global brands.

The Next Forty

The Industrial Revolution unfolded over a fairly expansive timeframe, from roughly the mid-18th to the mid-19th century. In the West, the benefits and challenges of modernization, industrialization, consumerism and financial advancements accrued over the course of a century.

China's recent industrial, technological and economic advancement took place over an incredibly condensed period of only forty years. How the country builds on this growth and modernization, continues to advance the living standards of its people and meets the challenges of being an established, rather than a rising power will have a profound effect on China and realizing "the Chinese Dream". It will also affect how the rest of the world develops in conjunction with it. The Chinese Dream, like the American Dream depends on Chinese people from all walks of life making, moving and buying products and services on an even more massive scale than we see today. New Retail is the foundation for China's evolution and growth and commercial interactions in the rest of the world will also profit from it going forward.

CHAPTER 2

New Retail: Born in China

"New Retail" was a term introduced by Jack Ma in October 2016 to describe a complete reimagining of retail with a focus on integrating online and offline retail. It was also one aspect of a set of 5 emerging trends - New Retail, New Manufacturing, New Finance, New Technology and New Energy - that Alibaba prioritized for its growth strategies going forward. During the same speech, Mr. Ma also predicted that the term "e-commerce" would soon go out of use. It would soon be an assumed and built-in part of future commerce and he said that the word would be retired internally at Alibaba.

But what does New Retail really mean? What does New Retail look like? How does it work? It's a merging of online and offline. It's a broad expansion of commerce as an embedded part of our daily experiences. It's a system that brings together logistics, delivery, warehousing and purchasing so that it can be done in ways that are cost effective and profitable for merchants and convenient for customers. In China, it's a space already dominated by a few tech titans who control these highly integrated platforms. These big platforms allow merchants and brands to make use of their integrated systems. And it's something every brand and company owner needs to understand if they want to succeed not only in Asia but anywhere in the next five to ten years.

But, how did we get here. Let's take a look back first.

The New Us

In a sense, we've entered a cyborg age, but not in the way we anticipated or the way it has been presented in sci-fi. Twenty years ago, going online was something we did in our spare time. Something to entertain us and distract us from real life. Even ten years ago, before the advent of the iPhone and the smart device age it ushered in, we led largely offline lives. Starting roughly in 2009, a perfect storm of innovation in technology, smart devices, computing power, connectivity, logistics and e-commerce forever altered who we are and how we live.

China's rise as a global manufacturing centre and then as a consumer superpower played a huge role in that transformation and its re-emergence as a global power in recent years has accelerated other transitions. China experienced a perfect digital storm.

Some of the key elements of the perfect digital storm included:

- the evolution of the internet into a highly global and accessible "public utility"

- the evolution and ubiquity of fast, affordable internet connectivity

- the introduction of smartphones and devices

- the global financial crisis of 2008 that drove more people to become savvy or unconventional consumers

- the introduction of "free" voice and video over the internet

- the evolution of mass social media platforms

- the evolution and ubiquity of digital products such as apps, video games and more

- the emergence of conglomerates that blend technology, supply chains and digital commerce

- the emergence of China's super consumers who bypassed traditional commerce for online retail, online payment solutions and digital social interaction

Now, much of what we do and experience on a daily basis is either directly or indirectly digital. We spend more of our days looking at a screen than at our friends, family or colleagues.

We work online, shop online, and are entertained online. We book travel, buy groceries, make appointments, order food, study and play games online.

Even our TVs are "smart", connected devices and data collection terminals. Networks, advertisers, device makers, game producers and websites that we access on our TVs are all collecting detailed information about us, all the time, every day. And if we have voice-activated controls, they're also listening. The effort to literally get into our heads is ramping up. As we go to print, Amazon has announced that they are going to introduce technology that works in tandem with Alexa to read your emotions. This is part of their bigger drive to become the global leader in digital healthcare.

Sure, we still take hikes in the woods and strolls on the beach. We still go to the movies, the theater, nightclubs and bars. We still shop in physical stores, visit museums, have meetings and meaningful conversations. We also still gather, bond, celebrate and mourn together in communities.

But for many, real life is now virtual and we need digital detoxes to take a break from it.

Increasingly, there is a digital us, a physical us and a blended online/offline us.

How Does this Fit with Retail?

Let's start with this idea: Retail is not a store. It's an experience.

In recent years, there has been much talk of a retail apocalypse. It's as if an anti-retail meteor has struck the Earth and ended all shopping, selling and consumption in a single extinction level event. The evidence centres on the number of stores that have closed and the number of retailers filing for Chapter 11 or shutting down completely. This narrative is common in the West, but the same can also be heard in China and Asia.

The problem here is one of terminology. The terms "retail" and "store" are used interchangeably but they're not the same thing.

Yes, over the last decade in the United States, Europe and Asia, tens of thousands of physical stores have closed and hundreds of retailers have gone out of business. But the history of retail shows that this is the norm, not the exception. There have been numerous retail disruptions over the last 150 years that resulted in thousands of store closings and hundreds of retailers moving on to the great cash register in the sky. What makes it different this time is the speed and scale of the disruption.

But it's not a retail apocalypse. It is, in fact, a retail renaissance. We're in the midst of a great flowering and revitalization of retail and consumption.

A Bit of Retail History

Like the 14th-17th century rebirth of art, literature, science and culture that marked the end of the middle ages, this change marks the end of a relatively short dark age for retail. We're now in a transition period from the Old Retail to the New. Retail is still built on some of the pillars of the past, but new pillars have been added.

Until the shift of rural populations to urban areas in the late 20th century in China, the 19th and early 20th century saw the largest and most sustained urbanization in world history. The industrial revolution drew people to cities. The correlation between urbanization and consumption is undeniable.

So how would these newly urbanized, middle class, modern consumers get what they needed and how would sellers best serve them?

The first modern retail disruption was the invention of the modern department store.

Department stores were as much about an experience as they were about shopping. They offered an endless array of products in almost every category. They were glamorous and fun. They were inclusive and showcased the four pillars of retail: price, selection, convenience and experience.

Then, in the 19th century, mail order catalogues emerged to provide a way for rural populations to engage in mass consumption. The Sears Roebuck catalogue offered everything from seeds, nails and ploughs to jewelry and artwork.

In the early 20th century, retailers transferred a mass production approach to mass selling. Chain stores and supermarkets emerged and grew at the local, regional and national levels. The first modern brands emerged and modern advertising and marketing campaigns started.

Retail underwent another revolution in the 1960s with the introduction of malls, a place to house many individual retailers, brands and department stores that would draw traffic based on diversity of offerings, convenience and social experience.

Sam Walton and Walmart shook up retail yet again with the introduction of everyday low prices, big box superstores and the establishment of operations in all parts of America. The days of having to travel to the "big city" to shop were over. Mom and pop retailers were hard hit.

In the 1990s specialty big box stores emerged and started denting the sales of department stores.

And then finally in the mid 90s e-commerce was born.

The E-commerce era

Many thought it would be the ultimate game changer and if you're reading this book, you're likely familiar with the history of e-commerce and its pioneers. Amazon, eBay, Alibaba, JD, Rakuten, and thousands of other smaller sites and specialty apps have all impacted the way we think about and engage in consumption.

But, as we write this, e-commerce still only accounts for about 9.9% of total retail in the US, 17.6% in the UK, 10% in Europe and 12% globally. The global average is expected to hit just over 17% by 2021. This global average would be much lower if not for one important fact. E-commerce accounts for 30% of retail sales in China today and is expected to increase to 35% by 2019.

But, even in China, e-commerce is not all encompassing in retail. So, if 70% of purchases are not e-commerce, then what is the retail renaissance?

China is innovating and exporting a retail revolution.

The battle between bricks and clicks, waged over twenty years, is over. And the winner is New Retail.

The change that New Retail represents is profound and in the following pages we will explain what New Retail is, what it isn't and why it was made in China. We'll also explain how to build your brand for New Retail in China and how you can apply the science, art, technologies and methodologies at home and in other markets around the world.

CHAPTER 3

The Pillars of New Retail

What makes New Retail so different from old retail is that it's not just about retail. It's about creating massive ecosystems with an integrated universe of services, products and tools in the hands of consumers. As Alibaba's Global President, Michael Evans put it recently "Alibaba is a little like Amazon, a little like Netflix, a little like Google. What is Alibaba doing with such a collection of assets? We are building a lifestyle ecosystem."

How does it all work together? Let's think of it this way. If New Retail was a battery, it has four charging portals. Its power sources are:

- Commerce – This is focused on creating and integrating as many online, offline, and virtual retail touchpoints as possible to create convenience and choice including O2O, B2C, C2C, social commerce and more.

- Digital – This is the glue that connects and directs everything in the ecosystem and includes data science, cloud computing, AI, mobile technology, fintech and virtual payments.

- Logistics and Supply Chains – This includes automated fulfilment, cloud-based logistics technology, cross-border and last mile solutions, predictive planning, inventory visibility and next day, same day, same hour fulfilment solutions.

- Media and Entertainment – Content is king and New Retail requires a constant flow of it. Content is critical to creating the retailtainment that makes shopping part of a lifestyle.

By mapping your strategy with the power sources of New Retail in mind, you'll find yourself thinking differently about everything you do.

Courtesy of Tompkins International, designed by Alarice International

These four power sources are what make New Retail different from traditional digital commerce. They're all are of equal importance and fully integrated. Online commerce, offline commerce, technology, data, logistics, services and entertainment work together to create an entirely new commercial reality and fundamentally change the value stream for brands, retailers, consumers, service providers, entertainers and marketers.

New Retail is driven by a perpetual feedback loop of consumer generated data that, when analyzed well, offers shoppers hyper-personalized recommendations for the products they want and the products they don't yet know they want.

It creates a new consumer journey, new expectations and new behaviours.

It blurs the lines between media, entertainment and retail. It's changing how we do business, how we interact with each other and how we fill our homes and lives.

New Retail also goes by several names. JD.com, in partnership with Tencent, calls it Smart Retail or Boundaryless Retail. Amazon does not name it specifically but has been a key driver and major beneficiary of it. Walmart, Target, Carrefour, Otto, Tesco, Nordstrom, John Lewis and Waitrose, Decathlon, Top Shop, Kaola, Pinduoduo, Douyin, Weibo, Baidu, Bytedance and Netease are also building it.

We will refer to all of this as New Retail.

Everything that makes up the ecosystem is focused on creating a network effect and delivering the four C's.

The Four C's

New Retail is built on the four C's: consumer centricity, convenience, customization and contribution. Most traditional online or offline retail alone doesn't deliver on all of these. But together, intertwined, they can.

Consumer Centricity

Consumer centricity is about putting the needs, wants, desires, aspirations, unmet needs and *unimagined experiences* of consumers at the center of everything you do.

The big shift is from being a company-centric organization to being a consumer-centric organization. If you're still putting shareholders, products, legacy systems and turf wars ahead of consumers, you won't last long in the New Retail world.

Amazon, Alibaba, Walmart and JD.com all put the consumer first.

The keys to creating a consumer-centric brand in China include the following:

- Spend significant time building your strategy around the cornerstones of history, language, culture and philosophy. These can be your greatest asset in building a consumer centric company in China if studied and understood properly, or your greatest shortcoming, if ignored or dismissed.

- Work from the consumer inward. There should be a large funnel for relevant qualitative and quantitative data to flow from the consumer to you before you start over-marketing back to the consumer. This information is collected through all inbound channels, pooled and analyzed.

- Create a strategy for centricity based on a consumer's lifetime value (CLV). CLV will give you a window into how your customer will engage with you in the future based on past purchases, digital environments engaged in, offline footprints visited, behavioral trends and competitive benchmarking.

- Use predictive analytics for realistic assessments of demand.

- Deploy smart, relevant loyalty programs.

- Consider creating a Chief Customer Officer role.

- Chinese consumers have hundreds of technology, retail, logistics, service and media companies putting their needs, wants and desires ahead of what's possible, feasible or profitable. The real competition in China is not over who can provide the best products, it's over who can meet the demands of consumers who are spoiled for choice.

Convenience

All the traditional pillars of retail - price, selection, convenience and experience - are critical to New Retail, but one of them, convenience, has risen above the others in importance.

Convenience extends to all aspects of the consumer journey in China so when you enter this market, you're serving a consumer has been conditioned to expect convenience in all they do.

For years we had a Starbucks on the ground floor of our office tower in Shanghai. We loved the convenience of being able to grab coffee on the ground floor and go to work on the 7th. Then we moved offices. There was no Starbucks in the building. How inconvenient. That was until we were reminded that Starbucks could deliver coffee to our office. Hailing a taxi in China's big cities used to be a unique exercise in torturous inconvenience. Then taxi-hailing apps like Didi made it painless and fast.

Payments, appointments, reservations and purchases are convenient to the point of being perceived as a birthright in China. In some ways, China is suffering from convenience overload. But, that doesn't mean you're off the hook. On the contrary. You need to make it easy and convenient for consumers across the whole spectrum of the consumer journey, from research, to choice, purchase, repurchase and evolution.

Make it convenient:

- to discover your brand and products online, offline and through peer, influencer / key opinion leader (KOL) sources.

- to research your brand and products at multiple corroborating touchpoints.

- to engage with your customer service personnel at the presale, sale and post-sale stages.

- to buy your product anywhere, anytime, any way consumers want.

- to search for, explore, engage, buy, sell and watch your brand on their mobile device.

- to find and experience your brand through partnerships and cross-marketing.

- to integrate your offerings into the commercial platforms that China's tech titans have created.

Use the tools and systems that have already been built for you by China's major marketplaces, ecosystems and technology players. Engaging with companies like Alibaba and JD.com isn't just about building stores and selling products online. The more ubiquitous you can make yourself in all of their habitats, the better your results will be. More touchpoints = more convenience.

Seek out partnerships, cross-marketing and cross-selling opportunities. Partnerships offer network effects for convenience.

Pop-up stores and cross border e-commerce physical stores are also a good idea. Shoppers can engage with products from around the world and then buy them on the spot or later from home or work.

Customization

Consumer centric companies take customization seriously and make it central to their strategy. New Retail demands customization of products, services, experiences and journeys.

Pinpointing what customization is can be difficult, but this explanation may help. It doesn't mean catering to the passing whims and fleeting demands of every consumer. It means that the consumer wants products and the touchpoints on their journey to look and feel like they were made for them.

Some product categories that are well-suited to customization are food and beverage, apparel, health and wellness, cosmetics and body care. Advanced technologies such as geofencing, proprietary consumer IDs, apps, AI and big data are needed for full online-offline customer experience customization. As for inventory, in China, O2O retailers no longer rely on massive, industry controlled distributors to decide what will and what will not make it onto their shelves. They also don't rely as much on human buyers. Data science, multi-touch point data collection, predictive analytics and algorithms are stocking virtual and physical shelves. Rather than having 20% of the merchandise account for and support the other 80%, inventory customization produces the mix of products that consumers want.

Contribution

Allowing consumers, through the use of technology, feedback loops, content generation and social media to contribute to the growth and profitability of a brand, product, service, habitat or ecosystem is what contribution is all about.

The network effect of ecosystems is the most prominent example of how consumers contribute to exponential growth. Amazon and Alibaba are who they are today because of the sheer number of users they have and their ability to collect information from them in dozens of habitats. Both companies are the first place many consumers go to conduct a search on a product because of the sheer number of products they carry.

Both companies rely on consumer ratings, feedback and reviews to shape offerings. The big players in New Retail have nearly perfected the art of allowing the consumer to shape their futures. Now it's time to allow more contribution from consumers to shape the value proposition.

The Four U's

New Retail, particularly as practiced by Alibaba, JD and Tencent, as well as several other big players, hinges on the company-wide and ecosystem-wide application of the four U's. They bring together all the elements necessary for successful execution of a New Retail strategy.

What are the 4 U's? Let's take a look.

Unified Channel

A Unified channel approach is the integration of all ecosystems, habitats, consumer touch points and technologies into a unified O2O operation that enhances the consumer experience, the consumer journey and a customer's lifetime value (CLV).

Even many companies that have embraced an "omnichannel" approach in principle have failed in one key way - the distinct channels they claimed to be merging were never truly integrated. It's a long complicated process, especially for legacy retailers, so, unfortunately, many companies left strong guardrails in place between online, offline, retail, wholesale, mobile and social commerce. Each channel has its own supply chain, its own marketing plan and budget and its own technology stack.

A Unified channel integrates them through technology, data, customer experience, product mix, KPIs and profit and loss structures.

For anyone who wants to succeed in a New Retail environment in China and globally there must be three moments of acceptance:

- That giants of technology and commerce have built massive unified channel models as a strategic end game.

- Your brand, product, company or retail operation must be built to fit these unified channel ecosystems.

- Your brand, product, company or retail operation must have its own unified channel model.

For example, Alibaba has many distinct habitats, but they are all integrated by technology, data, inventory, supply chains, and 700 600 million user IDs. An Alibaba consumer wants to find their favorite snack foods online (Tmall/Taobao/Tmall Supermarket), at Freshippo, at the local smart convenience store, and delivered on-demand.

All of these "channels" are no longer really channels. They are all just transistors on a motherboard that all speak with each other, if one or two go down, the system may still work but not at peak. Performance is not measured by how each functions and what it produces, performance is judged by how effective the machine they are running operates.

The more transistors you have on the board, the faster and more effective your brand and sales will be.

Uni-marketing (aka Unified Data)

Uni-marketing and unified data don't mean there's only one way to market, only one message that fits or only one way to listen and talk to consumers.

Unified marketing is creating the ability to collect data from the consumer across an ecosystem and use data science and predictive analytics to ensure that the right products are in the right places in front of the right people at the right time.

It's about ensuring peak performance in terms of information flow, inventory flow, money flow and messaging flow.

Uni-marketing means that you understand that Alibaba, JD.com, and Tencent are now marketing companies, as well as commerce, technology and logistics behemoths. Data science is the centerpiece of their marketing and promotions strategies and they will incorporate their own and outside media assets to create retail-tainment for customers they know better than anyone else.

This also means the merging of various online and various offline funnels and channels into a seamless encounter. It's no small challenge and requires unified data.

In 2017, Alibaba announced the institution of a unified ID that it uses to track consumers on all its platforms. This includes properties such as Youku (a video site similar to YouTube) Juhuasuan (China's Groupon), UCWeb (a mobile web browser), Taobao (China's eBay), Tmall (China's online marketplace for brands), Koubei (a local services company), Freshippo (China's New Retail supermarkets) and ele.me (a local on-demand delivery service) among others.

This kind of unified ID can track the consumer behaviour of someone who begins a product search online and purchases in a retail location. It can also track products that are purchased online and returned to a retail location, be it a grocery store, click and collect pickup site, smart locker or other destination.

This also enables salespeople at a tech-enabled store access to the same up-to-the-minute customer data that the algorithms behind an e-commerce site have, allowing them to adapt their service accordingly.

Your company must have a unified data model. This may mean huge overhauls, such as the one Carrefour has undertaken to centralize information in an estimated 50+ databases.

Uni-Logistics

Both Alibaba and Amazon have set a goal of serving two billion consumers globally. JD/Tencent and their partners at Google, Walmart and Carrefour would like to do the same. There's also a global race to be the first to offer global delivery of two to three days.

In 2019, Taobao reported that it had partnered with Chinese company Landspace (China's version of Virgin Galactic) to build 2 rockets that would enable it to deliver parcels worldwide within an hour. The claim, however, was made on April 1st and turned out to be an April Fools' Day joke. But given the breakneck pace of tech advancement in China, it was believed by many and the days of incredibly fast international deliveries aren't far away.

For the moment though, the answer doesn't rest in rockets. There's only one viable path to realizing this lofty goal; building massive, efficient logistics networks.

It's worth noting that some of the biggest and most successful companies in the world have made supply chains and logistics a competitive advantage, not just a function. To do this, many developed new internal systems and addressed their supply chains globally, regionally, nationally, provincially, municipally, locally and hyper-locally.

Thus far, JD.com has set the gold standard for logistics and fulfillment excellence in China. Consumers, brands and partners all rate JD as providing the best and most complete fulfillment services. Logistics is a major competitive advantage for them. They have unmanned warehouses where robots do all the work and they are at an advanced stage in terms of making drone and robot deliveries a reality. Alibaba is quickly closing the gap with major investments in improving their Cainiao Logistics Network.

China is also far ahead of the rest of the world is in getting the product closer to the consumer. This requires multiple forward operating logistics and fulfillment bases deployed in dense urban areas. Next day, same day, same hour delivery on demand is possible in China because of the commitment the big operators have made in hyper-local logistics, or as we practice it at Tompkins, distributed logistics.

In the US, Amazon is the top logistics player. It operates more than 250 fulfilment centers and its Fulfilment By Amazon (FBA) option is a competitive advantage for the company. Amazon Prime, which offers free, fast shipping, movie, TV/gaming/music streaming, unlimited reading and more, has over 100 million subscribers. That's 1 in 3 US citizens. They've also recently moved into ocean freight, air freight and last mile delivery.

New Retail is a world where consumer expectations are of the "spoil me or else" variety. A unified supply chain and logistics strategy is a must.

Uni-Technology

Uni-Technology doesn't mean there will be one technology to rule them all. It's about harnessing a variety of technology for the single, unified purpose of consumer centricity.

Some of the key reasons that legacy retailers have fallen behind are:

- Their legacy technology systems are irrelevant.

- They're installing $30 million dollar systems that are obsolete by the time they're operational.

- They fail to recognize the abundant technology solutions on offer to ease their digital transformation.

- There are too many people in IT departments with too much invested in protecting the status quo.

- There's a reluctance to try new technologies, fail fast if they don't work and move on.

The core elements that make up a Uni-Technology strategy and deployment are:

- Cloud computing

- Data Science focused on consumer insights and uni-marketing

- Augmented reality

- Virtual reality

- Social commerce engines

- Mini programs / Apps

- Mobile payments

- Financial technology services and tools

Unified technology solutions shouldn't be too capital, time or resource intensive and it's important that they are also modular. This way, they can be built up, taken down and adjusted easily. Companies in China must understand clearly which elements to outsource and which to build and operate internally.

Alibaba excels in cloud computing and commercial platforms that provide consumer data to retailers. Tencent stands out in the area of mini programs, which are apps that run on it's WeChat platform. However, China commerce isn't solely dependent on major legacy systems pushed downward by giant enterprises. Rather, tech from smaller, faster, more innovative companies pushes technology forward.

The New Retail Hierarchy of Needs

In a 1943 paper titled "A Theory of Human Motivation", Dr. Abraham Maslow posited his "Hierarchy of Human Needs" theory. The core of it was that people must fulfill lower order needs first in order to achieve a higher state of being. We make choices based on the needs we're trying to fulfill. Once we've satisfied needs at one level, we can proceed to the next.

Hierarchy of Human Needs by Abraham H Maslow

For a number of years, we heard questions from C-suite, marketing, e-commerce, and IT executives in the US, Europe and Hong Kong that went something like this:

"How can we sell more through e-commerce?"

"If e-commerce is growing so fast, why are our online numbers flat/ shrinking/growing so slowly?"

"What can you do to get us on the right track?

With clients in China, we heard questions like:

"My e-commerce sales are doing well. How can we do better?"

"Our e-commerce sales were doing great for so long but growth has slowed. How do we do better?"

It was at that point that we realized they were all asking the wrong questions.

The only question they should have been asking was "How can I be better at commerce?" Period. Full stop. Now that was a question we could answer, but not without first changing some mindsets.

They needed to flip the model from thinking about e-commerce first and save it for last.

The best analogy was Maslow's hierarchy of needs but we changed the model to focus on how to sell more by changing the way companies, made, moved and sold products and how much they had adapted their processes to a New Retail model. We didn't ask how to sell more through e-commerce. We asked how to make e-commerce part of selling more and doing commerce better.

At the bottom of this 4-level pyramid, we have companies with a very basic internet presence largely disconnected from the company's full range of processes and services. At the next level are companies that are beginning their digital transformation focussing on a consumer-centric model, unified data systems and updated and interconnected logistics and supply chains. On the level above this are enterprises that are creating environments that are beginning to blend online and offline services. These companies are learning how to mix the two to create new experiences and offerings. At the top of the pyramid are fully blended online/offline entities that are digitized from end to end with effective feedback loops, unified data and efficient, centralized logistics solutions.

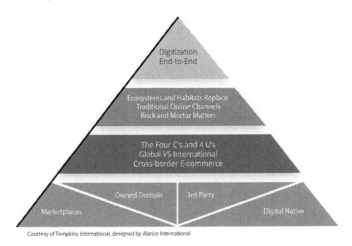

Courtesy of Tompkins International, designed by Alarice International

Now we've got the answer to the real question.

How to be better at commerce.

The retail and commercial world are being digitized across the board and retailers must adapt every aspect of their operations. Once there's acceptance for complete digital transformation, you can take action, reimagine your digital and physical footprints and sell more. This includes embracing global retail and doing more cross-border selling.

Those who want to capture the imaginations, loyalty, engagement and purchasing power of Chinese consumers must:

- conduct a thorough assessment of where their company stands in relation to the New Retail ecosystems

- identify and assess what New Retail opportunities exist.

- create a roadmap for how and when to engage with each new element

- decide which data science and technology elements to outsource and which to keep in-house

- decide which media, content and entertainment elements can be produced internally and which must be outsourced

- do the same as above for logistics, supply chains, social media and social commerce

- consider ways to leverage the technologies and tools that major players offer

- consider who to partner with to accelerate growth in New Retail environments

As Josh Gardner of Kung Fu Data, a China data science and e-commerce services company, puts it "focus on the real estate, the 50 square centimeters of the smartphone screen is the key to winning consumers in digital commerce China. Being above or below the fold can mean life or death. Win the real estate battle and you win the digital commerce war."

Putting it all together

The New Retail in China is made up of a few mega-ecosystems being built by its tech titans. They provide consumer-centric, convenient, customized experiences that consumers contribute to by using unified data, uni-marketing, uni-logistics and uni-technology. This allows consumers to become aware of products, explore them, experiment, purchase them and then re-engage.

How does this play out in practice?

Let's use Alibaba as an example. Jack Ma has stated that e-commerce will soon be considered traditional business and the term is now avoided within the company. Internally, Alibaba refers to its New Retail initiatives as uni-commerce.

It has many platforms but they're all being integrated through technology, data, centralized inventory, integrated supply chains and delivered to 700 million users. An Alibaba consumer can find their favorite snack on Tmall, Taobao, in a Freshippo supermarket, at the local smart convenience store or get it delivered on-demand.

It's up to them and in the palm of their hand.

Case Study: Freshippo

Freshippo (formerly called Hema) manifests all of the elements that distinguish the New Retail from old retail:

- the complete integration of online and offline to create a uni-commerce experience

- utilization of technology and data science for customer centricity and customization

- rich content-driven consumer engagement

- logistics and supply chain as a business enabler, driver and profit center

- hyperlocal fulfilment for on-demand delivery

- experience and entertainment built into the new DNA of consumption

It's not a coincidence that Freshippo is the leading edge of Alibaba's New Retail. Food, beverage, wine and spirits are the key categories to build all other New Retail offerings around. This is as true globally as it is in China.

Walmart, Kroger, Costco and Albertson's in the US are the leaders in grocery, food and beverage and they too are building their smart retail ecosystems around these categories. But for now, Freshippo is the gold standard for the integration of online, offline, technology and logistics to create a greatly enhanced value stream.

Alibaba's Freshippo is currently the most complete and successful manifestation of New Retail in China. It's a slick, slimmed down, brightly lit, modern grocery store. Or so it seems.

Alibaba made its first substantial foray into brick and mortar commerce with Freshippo. The company knew they had a revolutionary concept but were modest in how they talked about it and how they rolled it out.

No two Freshippo centers are alike. They vary in size, layout, services and products but the backbone of what makes them work is the same. Most are embedded inside shopping malls or part of large shopping complexes. This isn't a coincidence as malls draw a critical mass of shoppers and are conveniently located in key downtown areas of major Chinese cities. But the locations have been chosen for an even more strategic purpose, which we'll get to in a moment.

Let's take a tour of a typical Freshippo. A few steps in and the differences between a regular grocery store and a Freshippo become immediately apparent.

When we first approach Freshippo we're met by a semi-circle of small service company desks. Here we find a hair and nail salon, the service desk for a local fitness center, a dry cleaner and a travel agency, among others.

Once you've passed through the services area you step into the store proper. At first glance it looks like nothing more than a very sleek, clean, and well-lit grocery store. Not too unlike the modern grocery stores that started to populate the basement levels of Chinese malls in the 2000s.

Hopefully you've already downloaded the Freshippo app because the store is cashless.

There are shelves in the center of the store that offer a wide variety of domestic and imported foods, beverages, and other consumer packaged goods (CPG) and fast moving consumer goods (FMCG).

However the shelves are not stocked with an overabundance of brands. In the West there may be 100 breakfast cereals to choose from. In Freshippo, there may only be five. This is by design. The products that are stocked are chosen based on algorithms, sales volume online, ratings and data science. Also of note is that the shelves are stocked with limited numbers of each brand because Freshippo relies on fast, just in time restocks.

On the periphery of the stores are the cold beverages, fresh produce and chilled products.

A major draw and differentiator is the live seafood section. Here we find dozens of tanks filled with hundreds of varieties of live fish, crab, lobster, shellfish and other marine life.

What all the products in Freshippo have in common, whether they're cereal or live fish, is a QR code. Shoppers scan the codes of each product for pricing details, for information about the product and to put the product in their digital shopping cart.

Scanning the QR code for a live lobster displays information on your phone about where and when it was caught. Swipe left and you will see the safety and authenticity certificates. This is an extremely important innovation as food safety is one of the most critical concerns for Chinese consumers.

Keep swiping left and you'll see recommended side dishes. Swipe again for recipes and suggested wine and beer pairings. You can click on any item to add it to your virtual cart while also adding items to your physical shopping cart. If the store doesn't have the beer or wine you desire, you can open the Tmall app on your phone and purchase it there along with an imported cheese the store doesn't stock.

When you leave, the app takes care of the purchase automatically deducting it from your Alipay account. You can take your purchased items with you, schedule their delivery or take some and have others delivered. If you live nearby, they can be delivered in as little as thirty minutes.

You can also have the food and drinks you bought prepared on site. In twenty minutes it'll be served to you in the dining area. In some Freshippo restaurants, the meals are delivered by small, wheeled robots.

A trademark Freshippo visual cue is a chain driven conveyor system in the ceiling. It has feeder belts that rise from the shop floor. Employees fill bags with items and then hook them onto the conveyor. It takes the bags to the back of the store where they're packed for delivery. This is how Freshippo locations serve as grocery stores, food courts and local fulfilment hubs for online purchases. This makes Freshippo an important part of Cainiao, the logistics solutions company of the Alibaba Group.

Late night at the office? No worries. Order two energy drinks and a chocolate bar and they'll arrive from Freshippo in 30 minutes.

What else can you find at a Freshippo?

There are several restaurants serving a variety of cuisines; Japanese, Korean, American and Thai. There are self-serve draft beer stations, chilled self-serve wine cooler stations, and whiskey and bourbon stations. Automated vending machines make fresh pizza from scratch as you watch and the store is completely connected to Alibaba's online marketplaces, making for a full, layered, online and offline experience.

For all of the impressions and sensations that we experience inside a Freshippo, it's how it's connected to the entire Alibaba ecosystem that make it unique and a true example of the whole being more than the sum of its parts.

Around every Freshippo location, the concept is to have what Alibaba calls a "three-kilometer ideal living community" with the company's ecosystem providing people with a variety of services including grocery shopping, fresh and cooked food delivery, bike-sharing, taxi hailing, apparel and goods delivery, travel services and more. Their idea is to create communities that are empowered by convenient, online-offline services, technology and coordinated infrastructure.

Perhaps most interestingly, Freshippo is the best example of how physical footprints can drive digital commerce. The store is the draw that reconnects back to digital commerce. Sales and volume are healthy at the store locations, but Freshippo's ability to drive volume and sales in Alibaba's digital domains is noteworthy.

Freshippo also engages in what the company calls uni-commerce by making full use of Alibaba's Uni Marketing arm. This is the marketing side of Alibaba which tracks users across its system with an anonymized unified ID.

To give some idea of Alibaba's wide reach, it owns, is affiliated with or has investments in "China's versions" of Paypal (Alipay), eBay (Taobao), YouTube (Youku), Groupon (Juhuasuan), Amazon Web Services (Alibaba Cloud Computing), Twitter (Weibo), Google Maps (Autonavi), Fedex (Cainiao), Paramount Pictures (Alibaba Pictures), Manchester United (Guangzhou Evergrande Taobao football team), Uber (Didi Chuxing) and more. This list doesn't even include Alibaba.com or Tmall.com, which are online giants wholly owned and operated by the Alibaba Group, and for which there aren't really Western equivalents. Now, multiply that by China's huge online user base. Imagine the data Alibaba has access to coming from both online and offline sources. Imagine the story that the company's unified ID tells. It's unprecedented.

In Cannes, 2017, Alibaba's Chief Marketing Officer Chris Tung told Western companies not to underestimate how advanced China's consumers were or how much they already knew about their brands.

This not only allows stores like Freshippo to sell more effectively with a high degree of accuracy, but Alibaba isn't keeping it all to itself. Uni-marketing offers brands tools such as its Brand Databank, which is an online dashboard that tracks consumer interest in brands, their products, the success of campaigns, live streams or advertising allowing brands to adjust their approach and be more effective.

Freshippo manifests all of the elements that distinguish the New Retail from old retail:

- The complete integration of online and offline to create a uni-commerce experience

- Utilization of technology and data science for customer centricity and customization

- Rich content-driven consumer engagement

- Logistics and supply chain as a business enabler, driver and profit center

- Hyperlocal fulfilment for on-demand delivery

- Experience and entertainment built into the new DNA of consumption

It's not a coincidence that Freshippo is the leading edge of Alibaba's New Retail. Food, beverage, wine and spirits are the key categories to build all other New Retail offerings around. This is as true globally as it is in China.

Walmart, Kroger, Costco and Albertson's in the US are the leaders in grocery, food and beverage and they too are building their smart retail ecosystems around these categories. But for now, Freshippo is the gold standard for the integration of online, offline, technology and logistics to create a greatly enhanced value stream.

CHAPTER 4

How Online and Offline are Becoming One

Consumers no longer need to go to the product. Whether the product is a consumer good, bulk item, food, beverage, content, entertainment or an experience, it now finds the consumer. Neither place, time nor availability are barriers to consumers getting what they want, when they want it.

Consumers contribute to the brand by determining a product's design, use, experience and lifecycle. More and more, they control what's sold, where and how, creating a beneficial brand-seller-consumer feedback loop.

Data science allows for customization of the consumer journey, making it more enjoyable and meaningful for the consumer.

New Habitats

Jeff Unze is the President of Strategic Partnerships at Border X Labs. It makes the popular shopping app Beyond, which allows Chinese consumers to easily engage in cross-border shopping. He feels that the app, which combines the ease of online payments, efficient delivery and the tactile experience of being in-store, is a winning combination. He predicts that apps like it will "further concentrate sales in the hands of a few platforms and their partners that can effectively provide the New Retail experience shoppers will come to expect."

Once users get used to a certain quality of service, it's tough to go back to a clunky purchase cycle. Amazon Prime is a great example of this. If brands don't partner with the right New Retail partner they could risk isolation in the market. Traditional retailers could be put out of business due to their lack of expertise in online payments familiar to Chinese consumers, product curation, personalization and last mile delivery. The economies of scale some companies enjoy at home are their only moat and it's a pretty weak one when going up against large China tech giants.

"In the past, retail was either offline or online. Today, the lines are increasingly blurred. Boundaryless Retail is about enabling customers to buy whatever they want, whenever and wherever they want it. This means that it should be just as easy to make a purchase from your refrigerator as your cell phone, computer or an offline store and that the transfer of information from online and offline retail should be seamless so that there aren't any gaps in your shopping experience."

— Ella Kidron, Senior Manager of International Corporate Affairs, JD.com

New Finance

In China, digital payments are now the standard form of payment for almost everything from e-commerce to buying fruit on the street. Digital payments have an 85% penetration rate in Greater China. This makes paying for anything, anywhere, anytime with a few clicks easy.

This also means that technology companies are becoming financial institutions. Linking payments into the broader consumer ecosystems has allowed people to bank, pay, invest, and borrow in the same spaces that they shop and are entertained.

Cross border e-commerce has benefited consumers who can buy products from almost anywhere in the world, broadening their choices without having to deal with normal customs, duties, tariffs and paperwork.

The steady erosion of traditional global banking, finance, investment and financial governance institutions alongside the emergence of new ones will continue to have, an impact on the flow of global wealth, macro-economics and consumer spending power and trends.

New Supply Chains

Fulfillment is as much a part of the consumer journey as exploration. The integration of global, regional, local and hyperlocal supply chains gives the consumer the ability to buy products from anywhere and have them delivered to anywhere. They can have items from the other side of the world delivered to their home, office, locker, store, storage unit or refrigerator.

This has also allowed some brands to bypass marketplaces entirely and sell directly to consumers online. Examples of brands that have been successful with this model are OnePlus smartphones, Warby Parker glasses, Casper mattresses and Rent the Runway, with a 100% return rate for fashion rentals.

New Experiences

New Retail is not a transaction. It's not a process or a function. When done right it creates experiences and is an experience in and of itself. But it's not experience for experience sake. Done correctly, it activates immediate sales, return engagements, recommendations and enduring brand loyalty. The best experiences become a part of the consumers lifestyle, not just a part of their consumption.

New Retail ties together the products, services and functions of daily life into a new way of living.

"New Retail is about building a retail ecosystem that blends online and offline channels in a unified way that features the consumer. China will go full fledged New Retail as modern Chinese e-commerce consumers are predominantly young and mobile-savvy. It's already become a social activity, a means of consuming content and, ultimately, a form of entertainment. VIP has a New Retail advantage because of its position as a leading fashion and beauty platform."

— Zachary Ang,
Regional Business Development Manager, VIP.com

There are times when busy, two-income-earning, parents don't want to go to a store for the mundane or even the luxurious. The e-commerce tools of New Retail save us from having to.

Sometimes we want to make shopping a physical and social event. New Retail recognizes this and enables customization in the physical environment. Experiential shopping and "retail-tainment", fueled by technology and mobile devices, are a major opportunity for brands and retailers that will continue to evolve.

Some examples of experiential shopping in China include:

- self-service retail stores that connect to online properties and are made interactive through augmented reality, gaming and video streams, QR codes, mobile payments, facial recognition and a single user ID that enables custom experiences

- mixed in-store experiences including pop-up stores that allow brands to directly engage with existing and potential customers with gamification, sampling and selling

- using virtual reality and augmented reality to create a retail-tainment shopping experience

- endless aisles in the palm of your hand with the power to search for, view and purchase any product at anytime anywhere

- live streaming featuring "See Now, Buy Now" functions are available on some video and social media platforms

A great example of experiential shopping can be found in China at Innisfree, a Korean cosmetics and beauty chain. Innisfree partnered with Tmall to make their stores into New Retail hubs.

As Filipp Cai, General Manager of Innisfree China, put it, "Tmall's technology and experience will undoubtedly play a vital role in formulating our New Retail layout in the Chinese market. We have introduced digital, entertainment and interactive technologies in our physical stores, merged online and offline membership and enhanced consumer insights through upgrading our stores."

The locations feature:

- Magic Mirrors: These smart displays use augmented reality (AR) to allow customers to experiment with different makeup. Filters show what the makeup looks like on the customer's face on an LED screen.

- Smart Skin Analyzer: High-precision cameras can analyze images of a customer's skin, instantaneously generate a detailed report and recommend the best products for your skin. Scanning a QR code lets customers store the report in their Taobao account.

- Vending Machine: Using the Taobao app, customers can scan a QR code and purchase a facial mask at a steep discount.

- Smart Shelf: When a customer picks up a product from the sensor-equipped shelf, product details pop up on a touchscreen. This allows customers to learn more about the product before buying.

- Cloud Shelf: This technology is best for stores with limited space. It let customers see all the products available on the Innisfree Tmall flagship store, not just those on display at the brick and mortar location.

- AR Interactive Photo Booth: Innisfree's members could take photos with its brand ambassadors, popular Chinese boy band Nine Percent, using an interactive AR big screen.

- Claw Crane: By scanning the QR code on the machine, visitors could opt to participate in Innisfree's membership program and win three tries to grab a free sample.

Customers also had the option of making their purchases in-store or ordering from Innisfree's flagship store on Tmall by scanning a QR code.

The New Model

In China, official brand websites were never, and still aren't, important e-commerce sales vehicles. Instead, major marketplaces are the entry point for Chinese consumers. It started with Alibaba's C2C marketplace Taobao and JD.com's online retail store, and then progressed to Alibaba's Tmall and JDs marketplace.

In the West, the two biggest problems brands face with owned domain sites are:

- attracting consumers and generating a critical mass of traffic and conversions to make it a profitable channel. The great majority of brand sites cannot generate the amount of traffic to justify the high cost of marketing, selling and shipping goods.

- if brands can draw a critical mass of users, they're faced with a choice on fulfillment - slow and cheap or fast and expensive.

One of Amazon's great contributions to the development of New Retail was the introduction of Amazon Prime. It tapped into consumer's desire for instant gratification, became a major differentiator for the Amazon brand, proved that fulfilment is an equally important part of the consumer journey and set a standard of expectation on fast delivery that brands could not meet unless they spent a lot of money.

In New Retail, channels are becoming irrelevant. Rather than a focus on channels or the linking of channels, brands must understand the entire retail experiential ecosystem.

In a world where channels are evolving into a unified experience, e-commerce is not the end game. Not for Amazon, Alibaba, JD, Rakuten or others and certainly not for brands. E-commerce is a set of digital habitats that contribute to the New Retail ecosystem.

The new focus is on ecosystems and habitats, not channels and e-commerce.

PART II

The New Retail Titans, Technologies and Consumers

CHAPTER 5

It's All About the Data

We can't stress enough that data collection and analysis is the most important factor for success in New Retail, not just in China but globally.

Data science allows for customization, personalization, highly targeted marketing, comprehensive customer relationship management and more. As China's online marketplace ecosystem is now far more complex and much more challenging than it used to be, data science as the engine of New Retail is all the more important.

Josh Gardner, CEO of Kung Fu Data, a China-based data and e-commerce services company, says, "There was a time when brands listed items in their online marketplace stores, using what worked offline or in other countries, without much use of precise data. Being early gave those brands a big advantage and simply paying attention to general demand created massive success. Today that is no longer true."

So how do online marketplaces in China present key data?

In addition to giving brands important data behind the scenes, many platforms in China make key data public for all to see. Individual product sales and merchant performance data is posted on the site in the product's listing. Amazon doesn't publish sales numbers this way.

In China, brands, stores, operators and consumers can all see exactly what everyone else is doing and the platform is the host for the businesses operating on it, not a challenger to them. This has put competition on steroids. Platforms like Taobao have become places where brands have gladiator battles where the winner takes all.

China's abundance of data and this battleground mentality have also led to China being an artificial intelligence (AI) and machine learning leader. We'll explain more about that later but first, let's talk about something more basic.

What are AI and machine learning?

Artificial intelligence is the ability of software and the machines they control to learn based on feedback from the environment or a large data set. It's used to describe systems that mimic functions we associate with the human mind, like learning and problem solving. The hope is for it to save manpower and improve efficiency.

Machine learning is a fundamental concept in AI research. It evolved from the study of pattern recognition and computational learning. It studies and constructs mathematical formulas, called algorithms, that learn, change over time and make predictions using data.

How are they used?

AI and machine learning can be widely applied to various fields including natural language processing, biometrics, speech recognition, handwriting recognition and many more.

> *"We're hoping to be the best in China in terms of AI-assisted communication with our customers. And the experience we're creating is very personalized. I always say that no matter if it's search, advertising or something else, it has to be personally relevant. If it's not personally relevant, it's a waste of their time."*
>
> — Chen Zhang, Chief Technology Officer, JD.com

AI technology and machine learning can also be integrated into sales and supply chain management. AI can collect and analyze data from merchants and suppliers and then be used to help merchants optimize their product mix. In this sense, it functions as a buyer.

Then comes storage and delivery. Major e-commerce giants in China including Tmall, JD.com and Amazon have all adopted unmanned sorting systems. Goods are recognized and sorted by machines and robots, then transferred to conveyors for packing and delivery. Drones are also used for delivery. With the help of AI, manpower is drastically reduced in the storage and delivery process.

After goods are delivered to merchants, AI can analyze customer demands and preferences, browsing history and purchase records and recommend products that match their needs. It can also be used in unmanned stores. Cameras with advanced facial recognition capabilities can be installed in unmanned stores to monitor customer traffic and even study facial expressions to monitor reactions to certain products.

> *"Large-scale computing and data are the father and mother of artificial intelligence. Today, worldwide, companies that have the resources and platforms to truly develop artificial intelligence technologies are fewer than five. Successful companies must have both data and computing capacity, and also believe in high demand for AI. Alibaba is definitely one of the top three."*
>
> — Jack Ma,
> Co-founder and Executive Chairman of Alibaba Group,
> speaking at a 2017 internal company technology summit

After-sales service is important and intelligent customer service systems backed by AI reduce the workload of human staff and improve efficiency. With natural language processing and deep learning capabilities, intelligent customer service systems can deal with most questions from customers, make customized product recommendations and handle services like order editing, product returns and refunds.

AI and data analysis is also improving predictive marketing which determines which marketing strategies and actions have the highest probability of success. It helps businesses understand which steps and actions specific consumer groups will take and when. Data and insights can come from various sources such as be demographic information, purchase history data, web search analysis and more.

Who's ahead and why?

In his book, AI Superpowers: China, Silicon Valley, and the New World Order, Kai-Fu Lee discusses modern technological development in China and the United States with great insight as he has worked with big tech companies and seen things on the ground in both countries.

He asserts that China's innovation and startup scene is at a more advanced stage than the US. In the earliest days of companies like Apple, Microsoft and Amazon, it was people tinkering with machines or fulfilling shipments in their garages. People were heavily engaged with hardware and had to do physical tasks themselves because the machines they were making and the infrastructure they needed didn't exist yet.

This same stage is the one China has just passed through, except that it has a lot of the software and hardware tech infrastructure in place and many Chinese startups are still heavily involved with the physical operations of their company. This means that staff do things like going out into the streets to move shared bicycles, mobilizing armies of sales reps to promote mobile payment apps to street vendors and delivering food.

In the US, these tasks can easily be outsourced. This is especially true if the company has received adequate funding. Software startups are favoured in Silicon Valley because they don't require this kind of physical involvement and labor. They're seen as less risky and offer the fantasy of becoming wealthy from the safety of your dorm room. Hardware companies require a lot more expertise, equipment and a great deal of the supportive infrastructure for them has already moved to Shenzhen.

In China, things are too competitive. Companies are waiting in the wings to reverse engineer whatever new product seems popular at the moment. Brands rely on scale, spending and efficient physical work to stand out from the crowd and only the best are left standing.

Lee contends that being at this stage when AI and data are beginning to dominate is actually to China's advantage. China has massive amounts of data due to its huge population. This already puts it ahead of any other nation in terms of data volume. On top of this, the data isn't only about online behaviour such as purchases, posted photos or likes. Because startups have been down in the trenches, much of the data is about behaviour that has occurred offline. This gives the data a further edge. This offline data is the kind that is highly sought after by companies in the West that lack information about what happens when people aren't online. They haven't been fully involved in the logistical realities of their business in the same way that Chinese startups have had to be out of necessity.

As one example, Alibaba has leveraged this huge data advantage to give each of its consumers a unified ID. This ID, announced in June 2017, tracks their behaviour and purchases online across its various online platforms and properties as well as offline in Freshippo stores. WeChat also tracks users as they hail taxis, read the news, make online purchases, donate to charities and board airplanes, all from within the WeChat app. This gives each company an enormous advantage when it comes to personalization, customization and being able to assess the effectiveness of its marketing efforts.

If data is the new gold, China is the world's top miner.

Applications

Social Credit

The Central government is pursuing a Social Credit initiative which allocates an ID number to every citizen. Facial recognition technology tied to these ID cards tracks user behaviour online and offline. WeChat, Alibaba and JD.com are partners in the system in different regions of the country. In 2017, the government of Guangzhou began a pilot programme for virtual ID cards using the registered WeChat accounts of users in the Nansha district. Meanwhile, in 2016, in Wuhan, the local government teamed up with Alipay, an affiliate of Alibaba Group Holding, to launch its electronic ID card service. More than 400,000 city residents took part. JD.com's social credit pilot project is taking place in Suqian, hometown of company founder Richard Liu.

In Shenzhen, facial recognition and AI are also used to display the faces of jaywalkers on large LED screens at intersections and a system is being developed to send text messages to rule breakers as soon as a regulation is contravened. It's also been reported that the technology has been used in southeast China to identify a wanted criminal in a crowd of about 50,000 at a pop concert.

In Suqian, residents are not given a unified credit score. Instead, ratings are based on situations and circumstances. So property ownership details would not be a factor if someone wanted to rent a bike, for example, but it would come into play if they wanted to take out a large loan.

Artificial Intelligence and Machine Learning

One of the biggest applications for large data sets is to assist artificial intelligence and machine learning. It's hard to disagree with Kai-Fu Lee, who repeatedly urges in his recent books, articles and speeches that AI has, after a long period of research, development and niche applications, entered the age of implementation. Its capabilities are known and underlying foundations exist now for it to be deployed more widely. This includes everything from diagnosing diseases to issuing insurance policies. The book likens the coming transformation to the introduction of electricity. It will impact countless industries and affect everyone's daily life.

It's undeniable that data fuels AI and machine learning and no country has more than China. During AI's research era, elite scientific minds and resources were required. But now, in the age of implementation, all that's required is big data, computing power and strong, rather than elite, algorithm engineers. China's large data caches, which have a variety and depth lacking in the US, are key to building world-class AI companies.

On top of this, let's not forget the government's publicly stated goal of making China an AI power by 2030, its excellence in the field of supercomputing and China's large numbers of STEM graduates and students studying locally and abroad.

China has the advantage by a wide margin.

"In deep learning, there's no data like more data. The more examples of a given phenomenon a network is exposed to, the more accurately it can pick out patterns and identify things in the real world. Given much more data, an algorithm designed by a handful of mid-level AI engineers usually outperforms one designed by a world-class deep-learning researcher. Having a monopoly on the best and brightest just isn't what it used to be," says Kai-Fu Lee.

Lee's book also reveals that AI development will lead to huge industrial disruptions. PricewaterhouseCoopers forecasts productivity gains and increases in GDP of $16 trillion USD globally by 2030. About $7 trillion USD of that total is expected to go to China with $3.7 trillion expected to be gained in North America. If the predictions play out as expected, it's clear that the global economic and technical balance will undergo huge shifts that we are already starting to feel.

Facial Recognition

Major Chinese cities are employing facial recognition for transportation and security purposes. During Chinese New Year, also known as the Spring Festival, the world's largest human migration happens. This includes over 400,000,000 train trips as people go home to see their families. The technology is being tested in major train stations, such as Wuhan's. It's also used increasingly in order to board flights and as of publication time, facial recognition is being tested for payments at a station in Shenzhen's subway system. Passengers need to register their facial data beforehand and link a bank account to a subway payment method.

In 2017, Ant Financial, the financial services affiliate of Alibaba Group, introduced a face scan payment option that can differentiate faces even if someone is wearing a simple disguise or in a group. Other tech companies are also developing their own facial recognition solutions.

In Wenzhou, 20 stores on one of the city's main shopping avenues have been equipped with facial scan payment systems. It takes less than 10 seconds to complete a transaction by looking at an iPad-sized Alipay device. KFC is also known for its use of facial payment systems in China.

"Paying with your face" is increasingly seen as normal in China.

Smart Cities and the Internet of Things (IoT)

China's smart city program started in 2012 to encourage the use of technology to improve city infrastructure and services. AI and IoT is being used to help traffic flows, make public buildings more energy efficient, improve municipal services and more. Alibaba and JD.com have been particularly active in this area.

Alibaba's City Brain projects operate in a number of cities and use AI to monitor traffic, ease congestion and improve the response times of emergency vehicles. In Shanghai, AI is used to improve public parking. Huawei launched a smart parking network to help drivers find, book and pay for over 300 parking spots with embedded chips that transmit real-time information to a booking app. In Xi'an big data analytics are used to track population movements from rural towns to the city with the goal of tailoring public services to the needs of new migrants.

China's Social Credit system is also highly tied in with China's smart city initiatives. In addition to AI-powered smart parking systems and energy saving initiatives, JD.com's JD iCity is a big data-powered service that assigns social credit scores to individuals, businesses and potential investors and provides AI tools to local governments. Part of the data cache used to make these determinations is that of the 300 million active JD.com shoppers.

The United Nations, the China Academy of Urban Planning and Design

(CAUPD) and UrbanX Lab, established in 2018 in conjunction with Alibaba Group, are also involved in a UN smart city coalition that aims to pool global perspectives and best practices and create a global alliance of smart cities.

Smart Farms

Given China's large population and its goals for food self-sufficiency, naturally, it's found applications for AI and tech for farms and food production. Once again, China's big tech firms each have their own projects tackling the issue. In 2018, Alibaba's ET Agricultural Brain, uses Alibaba Cloud and AI to digitally record production details to improve yields, safety, quality and efficiency.

The company also has AI for pig farms. Each pig's vital signs can be tracked. It can also detect pregnancies, track their health status and food intake, monitor their sleep and determine their mood. This has helped Tequ Group, a Sichuan-based pig farming enterprise, to raise more newborn pigs, reduce death rates and increase income by 10 percent.

In 2018, JD launched its "Running Chicken" project. The company established a free-range chicken farm in an economically disadvantaged county in Hebei province. Chicken farms undergo 24/7 AI-assisted monitoring and the chickens are fitted with a specially designed pedometer. The system can also engage in automatic feeding, cleaning and health checks. Eggs and meat from the chicken is then sold on JD's platform. Blockchain technology is used for maximum quality assurance and full traceability and buyers can see detailed sourcing information by scanning a QR code on packaging. It followed this up with its "Swimming Duck" and "Flying Pigeon" projects in Jiangsu and Hebei.

Voice and Language Response

Chinese consumers are increasingly using AI for translation and voice commands. The Sogu Travel Translator receives over 200,000,000 daily voice requests, approximately 240,000 hours of data with a 97% accuracy rating for its translations. Over 500,000,000 use iFlytek voice input via its 400,000 developers in various industries such as smart home and mobile internet.

Microsoft is also deeply involved in these applications within China. It's Xiaoice AI language bot can engage in highly realistic conversations with humans. It's similar to Google Duplex, an AI language system that can make phone calls and schedule appointments without being detected as a bot by the humans it converses with. WeChat users in China can text or call Xiaoice for assistance or just to talk. The technology has also been used as a narration voice for children's books, as a singer and composer that learns from real singers it hears and as a news reader and journalist. The version of the technology used in the West is called Zo and, until recently, posted to accounts on Facebook, Instagram and Twitter.

Implications for Retail

Big data can be used to do in-depth analysis of customer data and create a 360-degree customer portrait. Even fragmented information can be put together to solve consumer puzzles and present retailers with a clear customer profile.

Merchants can develop a more comprehensive understanding of their customers, their demands, what attracts and retains them and use this information to optimize their marketing and sales strategies. They can provide customized, personalized service and offer different products and services to different customer groups.

The goal of New Retail is to ensure seamless engagement so that the boundary between online and offline commerce disappears. To achieve this goal, the first thing to do is connect the data from both channels and integrate it. Since consumer data is much easier to obtain from online platforms, offline channels have become the new battleground for consumer data collection.

Artificial intelligence plays a crucial role in the collection of offline consumer data. With the help of video monitoring, facial and biometric recognition technology and data analytics, a variety of meaningful consumer data points can be obtained and analyzed, including customer traffic, the favourite products of individual consumers, visit frequency, time spent in shop, purchasing process used and even transaction details. The sales performance of different products can also be observed.

Moreover, biometrics allow consumers to be identified individually, making it possible for each consumer to have a single ID that merges their online and offline data.

CHAPTER 6

The 10 Technologies That Will Change All Our Lives

The retail industry is technology-sensitive and has to adapt quickly to market changes and technological advances. Point of sale (POS) systems, barcodes, radio frequency identification (RFID) tags, big data, artificial intelligence (AI), augmented reality (AR), virtual reality (VR) and the blockchain are all technologies that New Retail brands have to rapidly apply. They help merchants get valuable customer data so they can respond to consumer demands more quickly and affordably while customers are catered to more accurately and get to enjoy brand new shopping experiences.

Thanks to China's huge consumer base, purchasing power, e-commerce expertise, ubiquitous digital payments and consumers' preferences for novel shopping experiences, it's a leader in commercial technology innovation. New Retail and Smart Retail are both examples of this.

Let's take a glance at the advanced technologies that power New Retail:

5G

5G is the fifth generation of cellular network broadband technology.

This progression from 4G LTE should provide faster connections while transmitting higher quantities of data. It's also a cog in the Internet of Things wheel as it enables reliable connections and huge data exchanges that can take place in the background. This will not only enable faster internet connections in general, it also provides the perfect environment for machines to be able to talk to other machines.

Cities that employ 5G experience less congestion in urban networks, especially for smartphone users, and have more home broadband choices. It's thought that other devices, such as smart AR glasses, will be enabled by 5G offerings and it's also been predicted that video viewing will increase alongside 5G network installations.

The acknowledged world leader in 5G is China's Huawei, which is highly involved in initial layouts of the technology within China and elsewhere. ZTE, Nokia, Samsung, and Ericsson also sell 5G equipment for carriers. Korea has also begun deploying 5G networks. From 2021 onward, it will become increasingly common until it replaces 4G as the standard.

Augmented Reality (AR)

One of the most famous examples of AR in action was the Pokemon Go craze of 2016 which saw people all over the world to go in large groups to locations indicated in the app to capture imaginary creatures. The game's AR allowed people to see creatures and game tools superimposed on real world backgrounds through their smartphone cameras.

When applied to retail, AR can help consumers better understand products and simulate hyper-realistic shopping experiences. Online retailer Taobao, the eBay of China, has a built in AR functions for cosmetics purchases which allow buyers to use filters to see different makeup styles on their face using their smartphone camera. The styles are often based on famous celebrities or key opinion leaders (KOLs), such as Angelababy, Fan Bingbing or Angelina Jolie, and allows them to purchase a package of items with only a few clicks.

The smart displays used in pop-up fashion stores, also called smart mirrors, interactive mirrors or magic mirrors, rely on AR, AI and radio-frequency identification (RFID). A customer can choose an item of clothing from a menu and "try on" the dress as her scanned image is shown wearing it on the screen. These displays have been in specialty locations since 2010 but have taken off in China and spread to stores throughout the country in the last few years.

In 2016, luxury jewellery retailer Chow Sang Sang developed magic mirrors to help clients see what different jewellery pieces would look like. AR apps can also help furniture retailers give customers a better idea of what certain pieces will look like in their home. IKEA has a mobile app that allows buyers to pick an item, then turn on the camera and "place" the selected item in any corner of a room at home to see the effect.

AR can also be used for gamification. A famous early example of this was when shoe brand Airwalk used augmented reality to sell limited editions in 2011. Fans had to download an app which worked like the Pokemon Go game, directing them to specified locations in major cities around the world. Only the people at the designated locations with the app were able to see the shoe through their phone's camera and buy them. The brand called it their "Invisible Pop-up Store".

In China, already in 2013, e-commerce grocery store Yihaodian also used virtual pop-up stores, launching 1,000 virtual locations overnight, some in iconic locations such as the Forbidden City and Tiananmen Square, as well as near Yihaodian's brick and mortar competitors in a very successful stunt that garnered attention and customers.

In 2017, Alipay used augmented reality during Chinese New Year, also known as Spring Festival, to allow users to find virtual red envelopes and receive the money from them. Red envelopes with money inside are the traditional gifts at this time of year. Users could see the envelopes through their smartphone camera in designated locations and capture them to get the money, coupons or gifts inside and add them to their Alipay account.

In some stores in China, you can scan AR-enabled shelves and an avatar will appear on your phone to recommend products to you based on your previous purchase and preferences.

Perception AI

AI used to need inputs from humans or other machines in order to operate but it's now at the stage where it can gather information on its own from the environment. This is called perception AI. Algorithms can now recognize images in photos or videos and identify audio. Perception AI operates beyond the level of merely storing data. It recognizes it, can derive meaning from it and produce it. This is the kind of AI being used in AI assistants like Microsoft's Xiaoice and Google Duplex. They can make phone calls to arrange appointments with humans and sound so realistic that the human on the other end is unaware that they're not conversing with a human. These interactions have been showcased at conferences and there are videos on Youtube of the interactions.

This also means that all the things we see and hear can be turned into data that deep learning technology can analyze and optimize. The examples cited in Kai-Fu Lee's book AI Superpowers are Amazon's Echo is listening to the audio in people's homes and digitizing it and Alibaba's smart city technology City Brain digitizing traffic data.

This technology will lead to a world where online and offline interactions merge and blur. It will be more difficult for us to define which world we are operating in. It will also lead to situations that previously seemed impossible, such as refrigerators ordering food from the grocery store by itself.

Virtual Reality (VR)

Virtual reality is an interactive computer-generated experience that takes place in a simulated environment. It usually consists of images and sounds but may also include touch or other sensory feedback. It creates an immersive environment and people wear virtual reality goggles to see it. They can also use special joysticks or gloves to manipulate items in the virtual environment. The virtual world can be similar to the real world or fantastical, creating an experience that isn't possible in real life. In 2016, the Chinese market for VR grew 343% year on year to $1 billion USD and is expected to grow to $8.5 billion by 2020.

In terms of buying products, customers using VR headsets can browse or experience specialty items, like vehicles, in a unique way. They can travel to famous locations without having to get on a plane or experience exclusive environments without having to leave home or go to a brick and mortar store.

How is VR being used by brands? Swarovski and Mastercard used virtual reality to create luxurious environments to showcase their pieces and allow customers to see what they might look like when displayed on a window ledge with natural lighting in a spacious, exquisitely designed home. In 2016, Macy's collaborated with Alibaba to create a virtual reality shopping experience on Alibaba's Buy+ VR app. It allowed viewers to visit the store's flagship store in New York, browse items and purchase them all using VR technology. And Jaguar Land Rover has plans to use VR headsets to introduce new models to customers pre-release. This will help them forecast demand, get consumer reactions, decrease design costs and add a fun, unique marketing experience.

China is now home to the world's largest virtual reality theme park. Located in Guizhou and costing an estimated $1.5 billion, it features some traditional rides with VR capabilities added as well as new, fully immersive experiences. It's been called a paradise for virtual reality gaming fans and has a variety of simulators as well as headsets from the past and all over the globe.

Live Streaming: See Now, Buy Now

Modern Chinese e-commerce consumers are predominantly young and mobile-savvy so shopping isn't just about passively adding items to their virtual shopping cart. It's a social activity, a way to discover new trends and, ultimately, a form of entertainment.

Since 2016, live streaming has been gaining popularity in China, and is now widely integrated with e-commerce. Both individual merchants and large brands live stream to showcase their products or promote themselves. More and more of them are adopting the "See Now, Buy Now" approach, similar to that of home shopping TV channels like HSN and QVC, where the audience can purchase the items they see immediately with just a few clicks using e-commerce apps like Taobao or Tmall and a purchase link shown on the screen. This function can be accessed on TV channels, through live streams on social media, in games and in apps.

For apparel, they also have access to a virtual fitting room where they can upload their photo and input their height and weight information to "try on" and preview new looks.

Mobile Payments

WeChat launched its payment system, WeChat Pay, during Chinese New Year in 2014 in what Jack Ma called "a Pearl Harbor attack".

During Chinese New Year, married adults gift red envelopes to younger people in their family and those earning a wage also gift red envelopes to their parents and grandparents. The amounts of money vary depending on the person's relationship to you, your income and where you live but are generally from 100-1,000 RMB.

On Chinese New Year's Eve, 2014, WeChat gave its users the chance to send money to others virtually using the app. Normally, red envelopes aren't given to friends but the app allowed people to post virtual red envelopes in group posts and the first person to click on it could get the money in the envelope and add it to their WeChat Wallet. People sent small amounts in this way for fun and to wish their friends good luck.3

> *"There's a rise in Millennials and tech savvy consumers. We asked those consumers, "Would you rather lose your wallet or your phone?' In the US, 75% said they'd rather lose their phone. In China, it was the reverse. 75% said they'd rather lose their wallet because they have everything on their mobile phone."*
>
> — Anson Bailey,
> Partner, Business Development at KPMG China

The convenience of being able to send red envelopes using the widely used app and the addictive game element led to an explosion of users for WeChat Pay, WeChat Wallet and the Red Envelope function. Up to that point, Alipay had a near monopoly on virtual payments.

Competition ramped up with the rivals adding more and more functions and making it easier and easier to use smartphones to make payments in all kinds of situations. China is now at the point where people in top tier cities don't carry much cash with them on a daily basis as they rarely need it. Even street vendors, buskers and small traditional markets take mobile payments.

And it's not just China. Mobile and cashless payments are also widespread in countries like Sweden. Although cash will never go away completely, virtual payments will become the norm worldwide.

The Blockchain

A blockchain is an open, distributed electronic ledger that can record transactions between two parties. It's a record of time-stamped transactions, called blocks, which are linked using cryptography and it continues to grow over time as more blocks and transactions are added. Data within a blockchain is resistant to modification and it stores information in an efficient, verifiable, permanent way.

One of the primary operations that benefits from blockchain technology is logistics. Since the data can't be modified, information added to the chain by manufacturers, customs departments and merchants can be verified reliably by all parties involved, including the customer. This allows customers to check if items are genuine and makes copying and counterfeiting more difficult.

Blockchain technology also means that just as consumers can trace items to their source, manufacturers can also trace items to their final destination and contact their end customer directly. Previously, manufacturers could only connect their end customers via retailers or the transaction platform but now they can find their customers more easily and provide highly-customized service.

Smart contracts can also be made using blockchain technology. The data is unchangeable once it's been verified and added to the chain so it works well for things like land titles and deeds. In some parts of the world, paper records of property transactions have been lost, destroyed or compromised. If these are converted into smart contracts, a permanent, reliable, electronic record can be accessed by all. These also have business applications as contracts can be enacted automatically and electronically, recording when and if payments have been made and enforcing consequences when necessary.

Shanghai, Shanxi, Henan, Guangzhou, Guiyang and Hangzhou have all issued policies to encourage blockchain development and Shenzhen has established a 500,000,000 RMB fund focused on blockchain investments.

Hangzhou announced its plan to invest 10 billion yuan in a blockchain fund and the plan for the Xiongan New Area economic zone is to use blockchain technologies to create a smart city. 41% of startups that received funding in China in the first quarter of 2017 were also blockchain-related.

Alibaba partnered with the city of Changzhou in August 17 to launch China's first application of blockchain technology in the medical sector while Tencent partnered with the China Federation of Logistics and Purchasing on March 18th to develop an industry application based on Tencent's blockchain including platforms for e-waybill service, transportation management systems and warehouse management systems.

Cryptocurrencies

China wants to be a frontrunner in blockchain technology but has initiated strict controls on cryptocurrencies and initial coin offerings.

In September 2017, China ordered the closure of all cryptocurrency exchanges and pronounced all initial coin offerings (ICOs) illegal. In January 2018, the People's Bank of China ordered financial institutions to stop providing funding to any activity related to cryptocurrencies and in February it blocked all overseas websites related to cryptocurrency trading and ICOs.

Facebook announced its intention to create a cryptocurrency that could be used as currency on its platform but there are strong reservations and objections from various sources, including Mu Changchun, the deputy director of the People's Bank of China's payments department, who has said that the currency is unsustainable without the support and supervision of central banks. Questions have also been raised about other key issues such as the effects it could have on economies with unstable currencies, money laundering and the use of the currency for criminal activities.

Although many cryptocurrencies, such as the most famous one, Bitcoin, are not in mainstream use and hover in a sort of financial experiment limbo, they are slowly developing and some state players are even contemplating or planning their usage. One example is Russia. The Bank of Russia is considering proposals to develop a gold-backed cryptocurrency that would allow verifiable state trade and commercial relations via an alternative to traditional banking.

Although no mainstream cryptocurrencies have yet been launched, it's an area to watch keenly.

RFID Technology

Radio-frequency identification (RFID) uses electromagnetic fields to automatically identify and track objects that have special RFID tags attached or embedded. The tags contain information about the object's source, price, dimensions etc., that can be read and entered into computer systems automatically by machines. This makes it, along with bar codes, magnetic stripes, smart cards, voice recognition and others, a method for Automatic Identification and Data Capture (AIDC). AIDC is also called Auto-ID, Automatic Identification or Automatic Data Capture.

RFID tags are commonly attached to goods and used in supply chain management and tracking. The tags allow machines to assist in the sorting and delivery stage saving manpower and enabling automatic sorting that's fast, efficient and accurate at a lower cost.

Retail stores can also benefit from RFID technology. As each product has its own unique RFID tag, any action involving the product is recorded automatically. In this way, stock control is optimized and merchants can track the sales performance of individual products as well as the purchasing preferences of customers.

"As a consumer insight professional, I'm fascinated by how new storefront experiences change consumer expectations. One of the key questions I'm thinking about right now is how luxury brands can use in-store heat maps, discreet-RFID tags and pressure pads and even-facial recognition to provide next-level in-store service."

— Michael Norris,
Research and Strategy Manager, AgencyChina

The tags can be attached to a variety of objects including cash, clothing, personal possessions and can even be implanted in animals or people. Although it raises privacy concerns, it's becoming normal in some countries, such as Sweden, for people to get RFID chips embedded in their hands to allow them access to their workplace or home, to store medical information or to use as a smart payment system.

Robots, Drones and Autonomous Vehicles

More and more work, especially what was once called physical labor, is being done by robots. Drones and autonomous vehicles are specific types of robots that will have a dramatic impact and be more visible to the public.

The automotive industry has been using robots since the 1960s with big booms taking place in the 70s and 80s. We're used to them being used to make cars. Now robots are being used in warehouses and supply chain operation centers to sort and deliver goods. They're being used to such a degree that there are now warehouses that operate without humans. Tokyo University startup Mujin has designed one for JD.com in China and will likely see more work in its future in Asia, North America and Europe.

Drone use to date has been minimal in many jurisdictions due to stringent safety regulations. China, on the other hand, has been very invested in drone deliveries and they have been used to make deliveries in for some years now in testing programs mostly for deliveries of medicines to remote areas, islands and to test for use in disaster scenarios and emergencies such as earthquakes.

Driverless vehicles are being used and tested the world over by various companies. Waymo, previously Google's driverless car project, began in 2009 and is now a separate division within Alphabet. It began testing in some Arizona locations in 2017 and launched a ride hailing service there in 2018. It has other test vehicles, manufactured by Chrysler, on some limited public roads in San Francisco, Atlanta, Washington state and Michigan.

In 2017, General Motors announced plans to deploy a large-scale fleet of driverless taxis in large cities by 2019. It has since hit several important milestones and Cruise, the company's self-driving arm, confirmed in late 2018 that it's on track to have the driverless vehicles on public roads by 2019.

Optimus Ride, a Boston autonomous technology startup that started off at MIT, announced in March 2019 that it'll deploy a small fleet of self-driving vehicles on private roads in an industrial park in Brooklyn with over 400 manufacturing businesses, and at an assisted living community in Fairfield, California.

Uber in the US is also testing driverless cars, freight trucks and delivery vehicles.

Smart drones, which operate without a human pilot on the ground guiding it, are also being used now. In May, 2019, DHL partnered with EHang to launch a fully automated smart drone delivery service for use within urban areas of China.

They are also being used in combination with robots and drones. Ford plans to introduce a fleet of autonomous delivery vehicles in 2021 that would be equipped with small androids capable of taking packages to people's doorsteps. Currently in testing, the vans autonomously deliver items to the correct location. Then a small robot with 2 legs, that folds down and rides in the back of the van activates. It takes the correct package and walks to the doorway of the house and puts the package on the doorstep. Then it goes back to the van and folds down again until the van reaches the next address.

Where Is It All Leading?

Technological progress is a major source of economic growth and China will definitely continue its innovation journey well into the future. Technology is central to some of the country's key national initiatives such as the Made in China 2025 plan, which established ambitious goals and benchmarks for technological achievement and independence.

Moreover, with its huge population of 1.3 billion, China has the advantage of incredible volume in terms of human resources. The country has a vast base of well-educated industrial, scientific and technical workers who can contribute to its rapid tech advancement. New technologies like perception AI are also hardware-centric and Shenzhen is a hub for hardware innovation and manufacturing so it's ahead of the game.

Tech innovation is also a driving force behind the digital industrial revolution. On the back of these advanced solutions, the New Retail revolution is gradually changing the online and offline retail ecosystem. It's helping merchants understand their customers better, while providing customized and augmented shopping experiences for consumers. And with that, New Retail is reshaping traditional retail in China and the world.

What could a retail experience that blends this technology be like? How could our lives change? Here are some examples and ideas of what a future with these technologies fully embedded could be like.

Healthcare

It's Monday. Time to get up. Ugh. Something's off. You turn on your voice assistant.

"Jeeves, make an appointment with Dr. Wong for 10 AM."

"Making an appointment with Dr. Wong now."

You get up to take a shower when your voice assistant voice comes over the speaker in the bathroom. "There are no appointments available at 10 AM. How is 10:30?"

"Fine," you mutter groggily.

As you get in the shower, Jeeves reports back that you have an appointment with Dr. Wong at 10:30 AM.

Later, as you enter the lobby of the doctor's office, a screen at the entrance automatically scans your face and a voice assistant speaks to you over the office's speaker system to welcome you to the office and tell you how long it will be until your appointment. When it's time to see the doctor, the voice assistant alerts you and a footpath lights up in the floor to show you the way to the doctor's office.

As the doctor examines you, he speaks into his microphone and his notes are written up in your personal digital health record. He lets you know your diagnosis and tells you about the medications you've been prescribed. A small hatch in the wall lifts and 2 containers with your medications in them are visible. The doctor hands them to you and you leave to go back home. A sick leave notification is sent automatically to your workplace by the digital assistant at the doctor's office and payment is automatically deducted from your account using the information the system has on hand related to your face scan and payment account.

Grocery Shopping

As you get your cart from the line, a message appears on its video screen welcoming you by name to the store. A list appears on the screen containing items that you have added to it yourself as well as items that have been included by connected sensors in your fridge and cupboards. A map is also shown pinpointing the locations of the items on your list zooming in on the location nearest you.

As you walk through the store, questions and information pop up on the screen based on your shopping habits, behaviours and preferences. "Would you like some popcorn today?" "This new sauce has 50% less sugar. Would you like to try it?" "This pizza contains no dairy ingredients."

You want to know where the cucumbers you're holding were grown. You scan a code on the package to find out they were grown in Spain. You can also see what day they were picked before going into cold storage and then being flown to your local store.

You head toward the exit and press the pay button on your cart. The items and their prices have been tracked through your whole trip by an RFID tag reader in your cart. The total is now automatically deducted from your virtual payment account. You pack the items into your own reusable fabric bags and take them to your car.

Education

It's time for school. In the Grade 3 classroom of Seven Lakes Elementary, the teacher welcomes the class as they sit at circular tables with their digital devices. On a screen at the front of the class, a teacher from Spain live streams to teach the day's Spanish lesson. The class answers the teacher's questions on their devices. She sees them in real time, acknowledges accurate responses and corrects others.

The students' devices and a database record the student's answers, response times and progress. The system automatically generates reports for the teacher and creates progress reports for parents upon request. The reports describe in detail areas where the student excels as well as which concepts the student is struggling with.

Then it's time for art class. The students open a drawer in the middle of the table that is full of kinetic sand to make sculptures. When they're finished, they take photos of their creations and upload them to their online portfolio before putting the sand back into the drawer.

After that it's time for PE class. It's the beginning of the year so students take a fitness test using special equipment that measures their cardiovascular fitness, strength, endurance and flexibility. The results of the test are added to their personal fitness and health records that were created when they were born. The records are accessible to healthcare facilities and include major health information including allergies, medical conditions, illnesses and more.

Then it's time for lunch. Students who didn't bring their own lunch from home can make it there with food from the school's garden. Some vegetables are grown there all year long using hydroponic technology.

Online Shopping / Buying clothes

Farrah is at a local shopping mall. As she sits with her friends chatting and drinking coffee, someone mentions a new dress they saw. Everyone at the table checks it out on their phones as she shares the link with them through social media. She checks the patterns and chooses a colour. The app automatically shows her what the dress would look like on her and chooses the correct size based on a body scan that she uploaded to the app 6 months earlier. She clicks twice to pay for the dress and have it delivered to her home tomorrow.

The app transmits the information from Farrah's body scan to the pattern bot which cuts material for the dress to her specifications for a perfect fit. The freshly cut material makes its way to the sewing robots via conveyor belt, has its loose threads cut off by hand, is packed into a box and sent on to the delivery department where it's loaded into an autonomous van with 20 other parcels to be delivered to her neighbourhood the next day.

Upon arrival at her address, a small walking robot takes the package up to her door. A smart locker at the entrance opens up automatically as the robot nears. The robot drops the package into the hatch, it closes and the bot returns to the van to complete more deliveries.

This isn't the world we live in now. Some of the elements are already with us while others are still in development but it won't be long before the hypotheticals written about here are reality. Is your brand ready for the future?

CHAPTER 7

How Alibaba, JD and Tencent Have Changed Commerce

New Retail aims to build an ecosystem that blends online and offline channels in a way that unifies commerce through digital devices, processes and flows, logistics, supply chains, delivery, media and entertainment. The three titans, Alibaba, Tencent and JD.com, have the same goal: To serve 2 billion consumers globally. To meet this goal, their strategic investments and innovations are aimed building this new unified commerce.

In this chapter, we're going to review their ecosystems and find out how they're using technology and data to realize New Retail.

But first, let's take a look at some common misconceptions about why some companies have come to such prominence in China while others have failed miserably. Plenty of well-known brands have taken their shot at China and have failed or retreated significantly. Amazon, Uber, Asos, Marks and Spencer, Airbnb, eBay and others can be counted in the mix. How has this happened?

Many believe that the Chinese government has rigged the field completely and supports Chinese firms while making life extremely difficult for foreign firms, forcing them to withdraw. While there is some truth to this, particularly during 2019's trade war, in that the government provides guidance in terms of policy directives, tax breaks and other incentives to local firms, many governments around the world do the very same, including the United States, so this is neither a full explanation nor a situation that's different from many others around the world. This explanation also ignores the many foreign brands that have been successful in China. Successful foreign brands in China include but aren't limited to:

- France's Carrefour, Lancôme, Chanel, Sephora, L'Oréal, LVMH

- America's Coke, Proctor and Gamble, Starbucks, Adidas, the NBA, KFC

- South Korea's Samsung, LG, Laneige, Innisfree

- Japan's Shiseido, Sony, Canon, SK-II, Honda, Toyota, Uniqlo, Muji

Some contend that rampant copying by Chinese companies led to their company's withdrawal or demise. Again, there is some truth to this, especially for small brands who were pinning their hopes on one specialty product. However, other brands, such as Crocs, have thrived despite being pirated rampantly, lacking patents to protect their products or being accused of pirating themselves.

Kai-Fu Lee, has a unique perspective on the issue, having worked with large tech companies in the US and China. In his book, he offers a more complete understanding of the issue. Obvious mistakes, such as failing to correctly localize products and promotions, pricing issues, setting up flagship stores in the wrong locations and the like, are, in his opinion, down to a faulty mindset and a flawed management dynamic going on behind the scenes.

Many American companies approach China as just another market without investing the necessary resources or giving their Chinese team the necessary flexibility needed to compete against sharp, battle-hardened rivals. They falsely think of China as a huge market full of consumers who covet their internationally known brand name. They see it as easy money instead of the cutthroat battleground that it is. They don't realize that, as popular as their brand may be, significant work is required to tailor their current products and create brand new ones to meet local market demands. Resistance to this process slows business down and frustrates local teams.

There's also a talent issue. Top talent in China often goes to local startups. They've heard stories and seen for themselves that joining the local Chinese team of a foreign company can leave one stranded, frustrated and bumping against a glass ceiling. The most ambitious young people start their own company or try to rise through the ranks with a vibrant local brand. This means foreign brands often end up with more cautious local hires and management flown in from foreign markets who are, as he puts it, "more concerned with protecting their salary and stock options than with truly fighting to win the Chinese market." In his mind, it's clear who the winners will be when the competition heats up.

Now let's take a look at three of China's biggest winners. They are among the country's largest and most influential companies: Alibaba, JD.com and Tencent.

Titans' comparison - executive summary

	Categories	f	a	alibaba	JD.com	Tencent
Social	Social network	✓		✓	Partner with Tencent	✓
	Instant messaging	✓	✓	✓		✓
	Photo/ video sharing	✓	✓	✓		✓
	Micro-blogging	✓		✓		✓
Retail & Commerce	B2B marketplaces		✓	✓	✓	
	B2C marketplaces		✓	✓	✓	✓
	C2C marketplaces	✓		✓	✓	✓
	Cross-border channels		✓	✓	✓	✓
	O2O		✓	✓	✓	✓
	B&M		✓	✓	✓	✓
Logistics & Supply Chain	Warehousing & fulfillment		✓	✓	✓	Owns a minority share of JD Logistics
	Last mile delivery		✓	✓	✓	
	Crowdsourcing delivery		✓	✓	✓	
	Cross-border warehousing & fulfillment		✓	✓	✓	
Digital media & Entertainment	Video	✓	✓	✓	✓	✓
	Music	✓	✓	✓		✓
	Gaming	✓	✓	✓	✓	✓
	Content & Information sharing	✓	✓	✓	✓	✓
Local services	Location-based services			✓		✓
	Food	✓	✓	✓		✓
	Travel			✓	✓	✓
	Sharing Economy			✓	✓	✓
	Entertainment	✓	✓	✓		✓
Finance	Asset Management			✓	✓	✓
	Lending		✓	✓	✓	✓
	Payments		✓	✓	✓	✓
	Insurance			✓	✓	✓
	Cybersecurity	✓		✓	✓	✓
Digital marketing	Search & browsing	✓	✓	✓		✓
	In-site advertising	✓	✓	✓		✓
	Analytics	✓	✓	✓		✓
Data Capabilities	Cloud computing		✓	✓	✓	✓
	Smart/ Cognitive assistants	✓	✓	✓	✓	✓
	Data mgmt & analysis	✓	✓	✓	✓	✓
Technology & Innovation	Autonomous driving	✓	✓	✓	✓	✓
	AI	✓	✓	✓	✓	✓
	Blockchain	✓	✓	✓	✓	✓

Alibaba's Ecosystem

Founded in 1999, Alibaba is the largest retail commerce company in the world but it's also a conglomerate that's engaged in core commerce, cloud computing, logistics, digital media, entertainment and innovation initiatives. The company began with B2B online marketplace Alibaba.com which focussed on facilitating exports for small and medium-sized enterprises in China. In 2003, they launched Taobao, China's eBay. Both were highly successful and as of 2017, core commerce still accounts for 72% of Alibaba's total revenue.

Some of Alibaba's key missions:

- "To make it easy to do business anywhere". It wants to empower 10 million new and profitable businesses across the world and create 100 million jobs.

- To leverage computing power to transform the retail landscape and build a data-driven retail ecosystem.

- To enable China's 600 million rural people to build businesses and sell their produce and products.

- To gain 1 billion new consumers/users/sellers in developed and emerging economies.

- To evolve e-commerce via New Retail, New Manufacturing, New Energy, New Finance and New Technology.

- To serve one third of the world's population and become the fifth largest economy by 2036.

Built on Jack Ma's vision, Alibaba Group has created an ecosystem driven by data. Its investments, acquisitions and partnerships are forged with the intention of providing solutions to real world problems and making digital commerce and trade more inclusive globally. The company's long-term strategic goal is to serve two billion consumers around the world and support ten million businesses to operate profitably on their platforms by 2036.

Alibaba's E-commerce Landscape

- World's largest global B2B platform created in 1999 as Alibaba's first business model
- Alibaba.com was created so that foreign companies can do business with Chinese suppliers
- The site handles sales between importers and exporters from more than 240 countries

- Largest domestic B2B wholesale marketplace in China
- Originally created for domestic trading, 1688.com is expanding to cross-border services
- 1688.com incorporates big data, tech, and AI in the development of the platform

- Largest domestic C2C marketplace with over 400 million shoppers and 800 million product listings in 2017
- While counterfeit goods are being eradicated, the platform still contains an abundance of pirated goods
- Drove eBay out of business in China

- Largest domestic B2C marketplace with over 500 million users
- Large selection of marketing services used for brand building
- In the top 3 most popular platforms in China and top 7 most popular platforms in the world
- New Retail synergy with Alibaba's entire ecosystem

- Flash sale B2C marketplace with over 400 million unique visitors
- Only best products from Tmall based on historical sales and service record are sold
- Juhuasuan is integrated with Tmall.com aimed to make it easier for merchants to transition to digital retailing

- Global B2C marketplace with 100 million overseas users
- AliExpress is the number 1 e-commerce platform in Russia
- Rapidly growing business in Southeast Asia and Europe
- AliExpress is the cornerstone of Electronic World Trade Platform operations and philosophy

天猫国际
TMALL.HK

- Largest Cross-border B2C marketplace with 30 million active users
- May be used as a platform for new product entry or premium SKUs

Double 11

Apart from operating its core commerce platforms, Alibaba is the pioneer of the big online shopping events China is known for. It's also far ahead of Amazon, which didn't launch Prime Day until 2015.

In 2009, it originated the Double 11 Global Shopping Festival, which is like Black Friday, except about 5 times bigger. In 2018, companies from a record total of 225 countries participated in the festival which generated $30 billion USD in gross merchandise volume (GMV) in a single day.

2017 was the first year Double 11 featured New Retail concepts, with the introduction of experiential shopping, see-now-buy-now events, an augmented reality game on the Tmall app that connected online and offline and pop-up stores featuring brands that have flagship stores on Tmall. The 2018 event was notable for its full integration of New Retail.

Services

Fliggy, formerly Alitrip, is an online travel agency (OTA) Alibaba launched in 2015. It provides diverse, convenient travel services geared toward younger travellers. It's not simply a comparison site as it provides a direct connection between airlines and their customers. This allows airlines to gather data directly from their customers and build their brand.

Brick and Mortar

Apart from e-commerce, Alibaba is also active in brick and mortar retail. Formerly called Hema, now called Freshippo, the supermarket is a showcase for New Retail, blending online and offline using a connected unified channel approach. It has physical stores in Shanghai, Beijing, Shenzhen, Suzhou, Hangzhou, Chengdu, Guangzhou, Xi'an, Wuhang, Nanjing, Fuzhou, Ningbo, Guiyang, Nantong, and Haikou.

Some examples of the chain's New Retail features:

- The stores do not accept cash. Payments have to be made through the Alipay app. Using a cashless payment system means the company can gather consumption data from both physical and online supermarkets to track and analyze customer behavior.

- Price tags at the stores are digital, meaning prices shown in stores and on the app can be changed simultaneously.

Data and Technology Solutions - Alimama

Launched in November 2007, Alimama is an online marketing platform that offers online marketing services to sellers on Alibaba Group's marketplaces. Alimama works with over 4.5 million advertisers and platforms across Alibaba's ecosystem and network, enabling brands to continuously optimize their promotion and data management capabilities.

Centered around data collection, analysis and deployment, Alimama is building a marketing ecosystem with various data and technology products that link the consumer-related data from multiple sources such as e-commerce platforms, localization services, online communities and weather services. Alimama works with over 4.5 million advertisers and platforms across Alibaba's ecosystem and network, which enables brands to obtain and continuously optimize advertising and data management capabilities.

	Key Features	Function Highlights
Taobao Express	SEO, Targeted Promotion, Store Promotion	Create traffic that leads to conversion with targeted consumers
Smart Dimond	CRM, Advertising Platform: Banners, Mobile, Short Video, Featured Stores	CRM service and advertising platform, which provides content in multiple formats that is effective for consumer engagement
Taobao Ke	Advertisement Paid Marketing, Collaborate with 50k+ media	Effective in navigating traffic
Pin Xiao Bao	Brand story and awareness, Inventory Management	Visually sets apart from other stores, provides a premium look that enhances brand building and awareness
Dharma Sword	Content Marketing, Targeted Marketing, Data Management	Target the right consumer with accurate labels and categorization
Uni Desk — powered by Alibaba — UniDesk	Marketing Solutions & Planning, Data Analytics, Brand Databank	An effective approach that provides data analytics through building a customized databank for brands

Due to the interconnectivity of Alibaba's ecosystem, brands can easily collect consumer insights across various platforms with Alimama's products and another uni-marketing tool called Brand Databank. Brands can then personalize marketing content and distribute it to specific consumer groups categorized into thousands of personas.

Uni-Marketing

Alibaba has a unified ID for everyone active on its platforms and can trace their activity across each channel and platform. This enables marketing and services that are highly personalized.

> *"We have more than 180,000 brands on our Tmall platform selling to more than half a billion consumers. The brands own the consumer experience, the consumer relationships, and the consumer insights. We are the platform, not the retailer. So when brands want to link their consumer data, inventory and logistics between their online store and physical stores, it's possible for two main reasons. First, the largest e-commerce platform is their partner, not a competitor. And second, they don't have to convince consumers to download their app. They are already have it. It's Tmall!"*
>
> — Erica Matthews,
> Head of Corporate Relations, Alibaba Group

Payment and Financial Services - Alipay

Affiliated financial services group Ant Financial now runs Alipay. Established in 2004 as an escrow service for consumers shopping on Taobao, it's become the world's largest digital payment platform with 520 million active users as of September, 2018. It supports payments of all kinds including online and offline shopping, bills, entertainment, education fees, fintech services and more.

As Alipay is used across Alibaba's platforms and at offline merchants, it contributes significantly to New Retail initiatives and bridges online and offline commerce, media and logistics.

"China's retail and consumer DNA has mutated in stark contrast with the rest of the world. The dominance of marketplace platforms such as TMall, JD.com and the rest of the Alibaba and Tencent ecosystems have grown with the rising middle class in China to become the heart of B2C commerce in China."

— Carson McKelvey, Chief Experience Officer, Tofugear

Logistics - Cainiao

Established in 2013, Cainiao is the key logistics arm of Alibaba. Alibaba recently announced its intention to build a global logistics network and is investing $15 billion over the next 5 years to support its ambition for globalization and expansion in China's rural areas. Cainiao's delivery network covers 224 countries and regions globally and 2800 districts and counties in China with about 230,000 vehicles, 180,000 delivery stations and 40,000 pick up stations.

Cainiao is based on a Taobao-like data-driven platform and connects e-Commerce platforms/sellers with partners along the logistics chain by providing data and technology to enable efficient and low cost delivery. Jack Ma said the target of its network is to eventually ensure single-day delivery across China and 72-hour delivery to the rest of the world.

Cainiao is currently the global leader in last mile networks, incorporating 40,000+ pick-up stations across convenience stores, individual and chain stores, colleges, campuses, community centers and pick-up lockers on top of the partnership with top 15 express delivery firms.

Smart Warehouses: Cainiao has announced the official launch of operations at its new smart warehouse in Huiyang, Guangdong province which is home to the largest population of mobile robots in China. There are over 100 AGVs (automated guided vehicles) in the warehouse, which occupies approximately 3,000 square metres.

Equipped with WiFi and self-charging, these robots are responsible for moving goods around. Looking not unlike a larger version of the Roomba robot vacuum cleaner, the AGVs can travel at speeds of up to 1.5 meters (5 feet) per second and carry up to 600 kilos at one time. Since the warehouse began operations in July, Cainiao claims that efficiency among its human workers has improved three-fold.

Smart Lockers

Alibaba has unveiled its own smart locker prototype but unfortunately, it's only a prototype for now.

The Cainiao Smart Locker is installed in a convenient location outside your home and sends a text message when a delivery is made. Once you receive the text, you can adjust the temperature within the locker to keep delivered food warm or cold. The locker is also expandable. In its empty state, it sits only a few inches away from the wall but can expand to 3 times that width to accept larger deliveries.

The locker can be opened via mobile, using apps like Taobao, Alipay, and Cainiao Guoguo or by facial recognition. Delivery drivers can access the box via a dynamic password generated by the box itself or via facial recognition. The box is equipped with its own camera and can record real-time images to allow monitoring of the packages inside it.

Cloud Computing

Alibaba Cloud, also known as Aliyun, is a cloud computing company under the Alibaba group. Alibaba Cloud provides cloud computing services to online businesses and Alibaba Group's own e-commerce ecosystem. It has 765,000 customers in China and over 2.3 million customers worldwide. It's the core technology that supports Alibaba's Double 11 Festival globally with inventory replenishment prediction algorithms

Alibaba Cloud offers high-performance, elastic computing power in the cloud. Services are available on a pay-as-you-go basis and include data storage, relational databases, big-data processing, Anti-DDoS protection and content delivery networks (CDN). At the same time Alibaba Cloud is committed to the research and development of large database systems and advanced big data technologies.

JD.com's Ecosystem

JD.com was founded by Liu Qiangdong as Jingdong Century Trading Company in Beijing in 1998. It started as a small shop selling CDs, then branched into other electronics items such as mobile phones and computers. After the SARS crisis led to a drop in customer visits, Liu decided to launch an online site to reach more people. It was a success. It became 360buy.com and then changed its name to JD.com in 2013. It's a Fortune Global 500 member and a major competitor to Alibaba-run Tmall.

JD.com partners with Tencent nationally and Google and Walmart internationally. As of June 2019, the alliances remain strong and active, despite the ongoing trade war between the United States and China.

The company's Tencent partnership allows them to reach over one billion internet users in China. It gives them a level-one entry point on Tencent's powerful WeChat platform and allows people to buy products on JD and share recommendations or promotions with their friends on WeChat.

Yihaodian is an online marketplace founded by Gang Yu and Junling Liu who had previously worked at Dell and Amazon. Walmart first became and investor, then took over the platform. It then sold it to JD.com in 2016. Walmart now has five stores on JD. As Ella Kidron, Senior Manager of International Corporate Affairs at JD.com, says , "Working with Walmart ensures that customers receive products at their doorsteps as fast as possible, whether they're sourced from the Walmart nearest to their house or the JD fulfillment center closer to their house."

In its partnership with Google, JD now sells goods on Google Express, Alphabet's e-commerce platform. Their store is called Joybuy and offers around 500 products, most of which are electronics such as keyboards and battery chargers, and kitchen appliances.

Google invested $550 million into JD.com in June 2018 and there were plans at the time to cooperate on retail solutions for Southeast Asia, the United States and Europe using JD's supply chain and logistics expertise and Google's technology strengths.

"From the beginning JD has been focused on building up capabilities and technologies and then scaling them. Now we are focused on leveraging our capabilities to enable brand partners, suppliers and evenother industries. This is what we mean when we refer to "Retail as a Service". It is about opening up our resources so that others outside of JD can reap benefits."

— Ella Kidron,
Senior Manager of International Corporate Affairs, JD.com

JD has rolled out its own New Retail initiative called Boundaryless Retail that leverages its ecosystem, including its supply chain and logistics solutions, to create seamless online-to-offline retail experiences that rival Alibaba's New Retail.

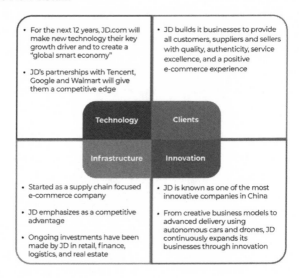

Currently, 90% of JD.com's deliveries are made within 24 hours because the company has invested a lot in its self-owned supply chain and logistics solutions. Many of its deliveries in major cities are made within 2 hours and its 7Fresh grocery stores can also deliver to homes within a 5 km radius in 30 minutes.

E-commerce

According to JD.com, it's China's largest online retailer and its biggest overall retailer by revenue. As of January 2018, had a market cap of 66 billion USD. It serves over 300 million active customers and focuses on providing

> *"There are three key elements of our business: experience, cost and efficiency. JD is working on so many different areas but everything we're working on is really focussed on serving our customer. For example everybody is talking about AI. For us, it starts from the front end. We really try to understand the user better than themselves so we can serve them better."*
>
> — Chen Zhang, Chief Technology Officer, JD.com

access to authentic, high-quality, local and international products and brands. This allowed it to become a retail powerhouse during an era when China began turning away from cheap, low quality, obviously copied items. This has also been its main advantage against Alibaba's Taobao, which is a consumer to consumer (C2C) sales site similar to eBay that has seen challenges in its efforts to crack down on fake goods.

JD.com has two selling models. First party sellers (1P) sell their products to JD.com at wholesale prices and then JD sells them to consumers while third party sellers (3P) sell directly to consumers using JD.com's platform.

JD WorldWide was launched in 2015 and is the company's cross-border B2C e-commerce platform. It currently has 20,000 participating brands from more than 70 countries through cooperations with other top global retailers such as Rakuten and Walmart.

As the 2nd largest B2C platform in China with more than 300 million active users, JD.com has become a top choice for comsumers who prioritize timely delivery over low price.

The fastest-growing categories are: Home Appliances, Fashion, Food & Beverage and Baby & Maternity.

JD.com has two models - 1st party seller where brands can sell to JD.com and JD.com sells to consumers and 3rd party seller (POP) where brands can sell directly to consumers on JD.com's platform.

JD.com is currently the frontrunner in the grocery and Food & Beverage categories with key platforms such as JD's 7Fresh supermarkets.

Launched in 2015, JD Worldwide is one of the leading cross-border B2C e-commerce platforms in China.

It currently has 20,000 participating brands from 70+ countries through cooperation with top global titans such as Rakuten and Walmart.

Brands in the Infant & Mother, Cosmetics, Personal Care and Health Care categories are preferred. The most popular countries of origin are the US, Japan and Australia.

Their bonded warehouses are located in 7 Chinese cities and 8 foreign countries. Their global logistics partners include DHL, Kühne + Nagel, Yamato, Costco Shipping and Dimerco. Storing high volume products in bonded warehouses enables same and next-day delivery.

Logistics

Logistics is the backbone of their business and JD Logistics is now a separate business group under JD.com. It has 12 million square meters of logistics facilities, including warehouses, fulfillment centers and distribution centers, which cover 96 cities and over 2900 counties and districts. One of the company's key aims has been to develop the smartest, most efficient logistics system in China. It leverages automation, big data, integrated AI and its broad experience in the China market to deliver to customers all over the country quickly and reliably. The company ships over 90% of its orders on the same or next day.

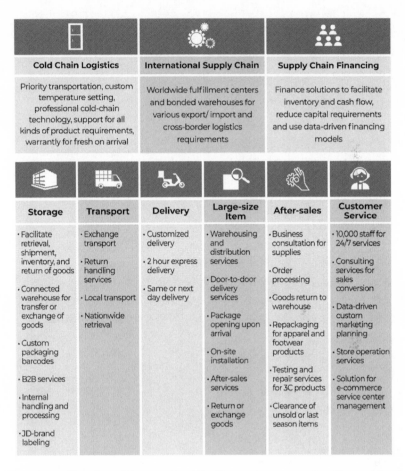

	Cold Chain Logistics		International Supply Chain		Supply Chain Financing
	Priority transportation, custom temperature setting, professional cold-chain technology, support for all kinds of product requirements, warranty for fresh on arrival		Worldwide fulfillment centers and bonded warehouses for various export/import and cross-border logistics requirements		Finance solutions to facilitate inventory and cash flow, reduce capital requirements and use data-driven financing models

Storage	Transport	Delivery	Large-size Item	After-sales	Customer Service
· Facilitate retrieval, shipment, inventory, and return of goods	· Exchange transport	· Customized delivery	· Warehousing and distribution services	· Business consultation for supplies	· 10,000 staff for 24/7 services
· Connected warehouse for transfer or exchange of goods	· Return handling services	· 2 hour express delivery	· Door-to-door delivery services	· Order processing	· Consulting services for sales conversion
· Custom packaging barcodes	· Local transport	· Same or next day delivery	· Package opening upon arrival	· Goods return to warehouse	· Data-driven custom marketing planning
· B2B services	· Nationwide retrieval		· On-site installation	· Repackaging for apparel and footwear products	· Store operation services
· Internal handling and processing			· After-sales services	· Testing and repair services for 3C products	· Solution for e-commerce service center management
· JD-brand labeling			· Return or exchange goods	· Clearance of unsold or last season items	

From its earliest days, JD committed itself to customer service. They noticed that most complaints from customers were about logistics issues such as lost or damaged packages. At the time, China didn't have a nationwide logistics system that could consistently support the kinds of deliveries the company would need to make so the decision was made to build their own from the ground up. That network, which today comprises over 550 fulfillment centers, covers much of China's population and enables same-day or next-day delivery all across the country.

This decision to build their own delivery infrastructure was a controversial decision at the time but CEO Richard Liu was sure that the investment and time spent would pay off in the end. Today, their logistics network is one of their key competitive advantages and the company provides logistics from companies such as Unilever, Oldenburger, and others.

Automated Warehouses

JD is the first company globally to launch a fully-automated B2C warehouse. Located in Kunshan, on the outskirts of Shanghai, its automated machinery, robots and autonomous vehicles pick, pack and move as many as 200,000 orders each day.

Delivery Drones

JD is the world's first e-commerce company to launch drone operations. The autonomous drones transport and deliver packages weighing 5-15 kilos and cover distances up to 50 kilometers. They deliver packages to rural locations outside of Beijing and in Jiangsu, Shaanxi and Sichuan. The drones land at designated drop-off points, where local village promoters pick them up and take them to customers.

As of early 2019, JD is building 150 drone airports, has a fleet of around 50 drones in operation and has the goal of developing drones that can carry up to one ton by 2020.

Autonomous Delivery Vehicles

After extensive testing in campus environments, JD has launched autonomous delivery vehicles in Beijing, Tianjian, Shanghai and Guangzhou. The driverless vehicles operate at a top speed of 15 kilometers per hour and can carry 30 parcels at once. The vehicles can handle open road driving, avoid any barriers on the road and obey traffic lights. JD is planning to expand its delivery fleet to more cities in the near future.

Unmanned Convenience Stores

To battle against Alibaba in brick-and-mortar, JD has partnered with real estate developer China Overseas Land & Investment Ltd (COLI) to open hundreds of unmanned convenience stores in China in 2018. The first store opened in Yantai, and other stores have been launched in cities such as Beijing, Dalian, Suqian, Xian and Tianjin.

The goal for unmanned stores is to provide a seamless, flexible shopping experience for consumers. They're embedded with the latest cutting-edge technology. For instance, cameras in the ceiling use facial recognition technology to recognize customers. Store access is through the JD app, a connection to the user's bank account, online payment option or credit card and the facial recognition cameras. The cameras also track customer movements and generate heat maps showing their product preferences. This helps store owners to stock efficiently. In addition, there are smart ad screens in the store leveraging this tech to show personalized ads. Products are tracked with RFID tags and readers.

These unmanned stores can handle an average daily customer flow of around 1,000 and expect repeat purchase rates of 70%. As part of its global expansion, JD brought its unmanned store concept to Indonesia in August 2018, marking the first time it unveiled one outside of China.

Online Merge Offline (OMO) Initiatives

JD's OMO initiatives boost and leverage their logistics network and capabilities and build their Boundaryless Retail ecosystem.

7 Fresh

This fresh food supermarket was launched by JD.com in Beijing in early January 2018. The store has 4,000 square metres of floor space and smart carts that guide shoppers to their desired aisles. It provides delivery to users within a 5km radius in 30 minutes. The supermarkets are on the frontline in JD's OMO and brick and mortar battle with Alibaba. It offers consumers rapid delivery and a diverse variety of products. The stores cover tier 3 and tier 4 cities, and the availability of both online and offline services increases the coverage of F&B brands to access more consumers, especially in rural areas.

Dada - JD Daojia

This OMO initiative by JD offers consumers the option of 1 hour delivery service on the online purchase of groceries, flowers, medicine and health supplements. The online grocery stores, run by JD with participation and investment from Walmart, Carrefour and urban delivery service company Dada. It covers more than 400 major cities across China, serving not only 50 million individual users but also over 1.2 million merchants with a peak of 10 million daily orders.

Tencent's Ecosystem

Headquartered in Shenzhen, China, and founded in 1998, Tencent is an internet-based technology and cultural enterprise. In January, 2018, Tencent became the newest member of the 500 billion USD market valuation club, alongside Apple, Google parent company Alphabet, Microsoft, Amazon and Facebook and at one point, was valued as the world's most valuable social network company.

Tencent operates a multi-layer ecosystem where each layer is independently developed, expanded and connected to the other layers. With messaging and social media at its core, it also has a large stake in gaming, interactive entertainment, social media enabled e-commerce and its own payment system. It also has strategic partnerships with and investments in business entities across different industries.

Target

The 7 tools, 5 areas and 3 roles add up to Tencent offering an **Internet Plus** experience and enabling people to use the company's services as a digital assistant.

3 Roles

Tencent is assuming roles as **"connector"**, **"digital tool box"**, and e**cosystem builder/ co-developer** for all business partners as well as brands/ enterprises across all industry sectors.

5 Areas

Tencent is upgrading five areas, including **municipal services, consumption, manufacturing services, health,** and **environmental protection.**

7 Tools

Tencent concentrates on developing 7 tools, including **public accounts, mini programs, mobile payments, social media advertising, security, enterprise WeChat,** as well as **technology** (big data, AI, and cloud computing).

Tencent operates a multi-layer ecosystem where each layer is independently developed and externally expanded while synergized with each other to achieve Tencent's ultimate goal.

Technology is the foundation to support the development of the outer layers, with social as its core business, rapidly growing interactive entertainment, as well as strategic partnership with business entitles across different industry sectors.

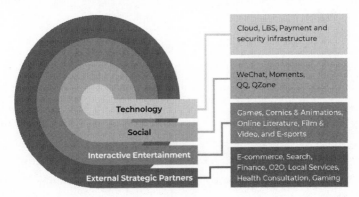

Technology — Cloud, LBS, Payment and security infrastructure

Social — WeChat, Moments, QQ, QZone

Interactive Entertainment — Games, Comics & Animations, Online Literature, Film & Video, and E-sports

External Strategic Partners — E-commerce, Search, Finance, O2O, Local Services, Health Consultation, Gaming

Social

Tencent's social platforms, QQ and WeChat, are key to its ecosystem. Launched as messaging and social media solutions, QQ and WeChat serve Tencent differently in terms roles but both aim to drive traffic into Tencent's other products and services, such as gaming and video products.

QQ

As China's first hugely popular messaging service, QQ shaped the development of China's internet and its mobile web. Despite being launched all the way back in 1999 (5 years before Facebook), QQ has survived the test of time. Targeting the younger generation, QQ introduces consumers to Tencent's ecosystem. It offers basic functions and services, such as messaging, gaming, public sharing and live streaming. Tencent prefers all-in-one apps that can be easily used on mobile devices.

As the first product released by Tencent, QQ hit one million users in its first year and 50 million in its second. By its tenth year, in 2008, the startup had 856 million total users, a record of 45.3 million simultaneous online users, and more quarterly income than the next two largest Chinese internet companies (Alibaba and Baidu) put together. Today, QQ still has 850 million active monthly users – more than double the number Twitter claims.

Tencent Weibo

The word weibo translates as microblog. Most people don't remember that Tencent also tried to launch its own microblog in 2010. Tencent Weibo's interface was very similar to Sina Weibo's and it was also competing internally with Tencent's Qzone blog. Both got traffic from QQ, but Tencent Weibo was never able to pick up speed. In 2014, Tencent announced it would discontinue Tencent Weibo. This was not a huge loss however as WeChat was already becoming the dominant social network in China.

WeChat

Tencent has grown WeChat into an all-inclusive app that's able to cater to most user needs all within one platform. Users can communicate, share links, post updates, play games, find news, pay bills, book tickets, hail and pay for taxis, shop and engage in e-commerce. Outside of gaming, WeChat is a primary driver for Tencent's revenue from products and services in many other segments.

WeChat is an open platform and embeds offers and services from its partners. This gives Tencent access to consumer data, and assists Tencent in launching new services to target a specific consumers' lifestyles. WeChat also has official accounts and mini programs for brands, enterprises and government bureaus.

An official account connects brands and retailers to consumers. According to WeChat, there are 20 million official accounts and 3.5 million active official accounts.

In November, 2018, China's Department of Internet Content asked platforms to limit the number of public accounts registered by the same person or business on the same platform. So now, individuals can register a maximum of 1 official WeChat account per person. Enterprises can normally register a maximum of 2 official accounts but can request more. Requests will be reviewed by both WeChat and the Department of Internet Content for approval.

Mini programs focus on transactions and services for online and offline services, including catering, retail, transportation, medical, education, e-commerce and online tools. At the start of 2018, 50% of WeChat's monthly active users, about 472 million users, were using mini programs. Mini programs are WeChat's primary O2O integration tool and form the foundation of Tencent's Smart Retail strategy, which is its counterpart and rival to Alibaba's New Retail.

Smart Retail

As WeChat expands its functions and features, Tencent is investing in strategic partnerships in various industries to form its own version of New Retail, which it calls Smart Retail.

Similar to New Retail, it's focused on eliminating the border between online and offline using digital technologies to boost retail and connect people, goods, and places. Tencent emphasizes its role as a digital assistant improving transactions for individuals and brands through mini programs, official accounts, payment solutions, cloud computing and AI.

To compete with Alibaba, Tencent has entered into a partnership with JD.com and both parties have also invested in Vipshop to further strengthen their position in e-commerce. In terms of brick and mortar, Tencent and JD.com have invested in or developed supermarkets. In addition, Tencent has engaged in acquisitions to expand its role in areas such as food delivery, transportation and health consultation.

Since Tencent began to cooperate with industries using WeChat Pay in 2014, the tech giant has continuously developed tools for retail enterprises through Tencent Cloud, social advertisements and, more recently, mini programs to connect people and businesses.

On May 20, 2018, in Shanghai, Carrefour opened a new Chinese outlet that leveraged Tencent's technology and the internet firm's huge user base to showcase smart retail. Called Le Marché, it was Carrefour's first smart store in China. It offers 25,000 product types, mostly food, and customers can pay for their purchases with their WeChat accounts by scanning a QR code or enabling payments with facial recognition technology.

Entertainment

In recent years, Tencent has focused on content creation for games, comics and animation, online literature, film and e-sports. Tencent already owns

China's three largest music apps by installment base – QQ Music, Kugou and Kuwo – where a combined 700 million monthly active users are not only listening to domestic hits but international stars such as Katy Perry and Rihanna.

When it comes to film and television shows, Tencent is modeling itself after Disney, seeking to emulate franchise films with long-lasting appeal such as Star Wars or The Avengers. And the company knows where they will come from; its online books division. China Literature Group claims to own almost 50% of the country's e-reading market.

The final building block in its IP adaptation chain is video games. Tencent is the world's largest video game publisher and games routinely contribute to more than half of its revenues.

Fighter of Destiny, an e-book published by the China Literature Group in 2014, is just one property being used in this way. It was adapted into a very successful TV series starring actor and idol Lu Han in 2017. As of January 2018, the series had gotten an estimated 30 billion views. A related smartphone game is likely to go online in 2019, with more than 10 million users already signing up during pre-registration. The estimated revenue from the series so far, including book, TV series and gaming sales is about 30 billion RMB ($4.5 billion USD).

Technology

Tencent Cloud powers all of its product and service offerings and its cloud solutions act as a growth driver along with its payment business, to target the public and private sector. Among other things, Tencent's cloud enables its location-based services (LBS) to process and analyze terabytes of real-time location and logistics data from internal and external sources. This data can then be used to integrate the user's online and offline experience and bring smart retail to life.

Security is a focus area for the public sector. Tencent's cloud network is the first choice with many retail brands in China due to its speed, power, coverage, and safety. As of December 2017, Tencent Cloud was running more than 12,000 virtual machines spread across seven data centers in four regions, including one in Silicon Valley, and managing over 300 services.

WeChat Pay

In 2018, 688 million people used WeChat hongbao to send lucky money in virtual red envelopes, according to WeChat's New Year's Eve big data. Because of WeChat's social network DNA, WeChat Pay was first created just to enable peer to peer (P2P) money transfers and in-app purchases. However, as mobile commerce took off and reshaped lifestyles, WeChat Pay quickly expanded its features and started competing with Alipay in many areas. WeChat Pay is now used for many kinds of transactions but isn't as strong as Alipay in some aspects of financial services.

Although Tencent wasn't established as an e-commerce venture, Meilishuo (a fashion and beauty Pinterest-style e-commerce site), Dianping (similar to Groupon) and JD.com are connected on WeChat Pay thanks to strategic investments and partnerships. WeChat Pay also brought in Meituan as a partner for food delivery services and 58.com, the Craigslist of China, for handyman services.

WeChat Pay can also handle booking doctor appointments, paying for utilities, checking social security information, filing taxes, paying at gas stations, paying traffic tickets, and paying postal charges just to name a few.

WeChat Pay can also be used offline by using QR codes at brick-and-mortar stores, live events, vending machines, restaurants, and hotels. It currently claims to have over 900 million active users who use WeChat Pay about 30 times a month.

Taking Sides

The advantage in China is that once plugged in to these platforms, brands can get access to information about their consumers to help them gain insight into their preferences and behaviour. And the platform itself is not their competitor with their own private label goods.

The disadvantage in China is that the Alibaba and Tencent+JD ecosystems cover so many aspects of social life that they leave very little room for competitors. Due to differences in their payment systems, logistics solutions, social media and big data platforms, retailers in the brick-and-mortar world have to take a side or be left out of the game completely.

CHAPTER 8

Modern Chinese Consumers at a Glance

China, with a population of over 1.3 billion, tops the board with the world's largest population and has the world's second largest economy. It's a market full of potential. Consumption in China is expected to grow to 6.1 trillion USD by 2021. Although estimates have been tempered by recent tariff and trade disagreements, China's standard of living is still expected to keep increasing and the country still has large segments of the population that are underserved. 70% of Chinese people live in smaller cities and rural areas. Reports indicate that over 50% of sales from the Luxury Pavilion in Alibaba's Tmall are from these customers who live outside Tier 1 and 2 cities. On top of this, by 2021, 70% of spending is expected to come from China's Millennials in the 18-35 year age group.

Understanding the mindset and preferences of Chinese consumers, and how they relate to New Retail, are the keys to success in the China market.

What are they really like?

While old ideas and stereotypes may persist, the truth is Chinese consumers, especially those in top tier cities, are the most sophisticated and spoiled in the world. The China market is currently flooded with a wide variety of domestic and foreign brands offering a vast array of products. However, with increasing purchasing power, there's still an eagerness for novelty and even more quality choices.

> *"Everyone knows Alibaba as an e-commerce company but even though China has the highest share of e-commerce to total retail in the world, more than 80% of retail is still traditional brick and mortar. We know consumers don't see the world in terms of online or offline, so brands and retailers shouldn't either."*
>
> — Erica Matthews, Head of Corporate Relations,
> Alibaba Group

This is why most Chinese consumers, especially those in first and second tier cities, prioritize product quality. They expect high calibre personalized products and services that are reasonably priced. They're also accustomed to quick turnarounds so they also want them fast.

Having said that, it's not realistic to describe all Chinese consumers as a whole. There are a variety of consumer types and markets within China and to understand Chinese consumers more deeply, we need to divide them into different consumer groups. Each of them has their own characteristics and purchasing preferences. Let's take a dive into today's most significant consumer groups.

The 2018 book China's Evolving Consumers: 8 Intimate Portraits, edited by Tom Nunlist, has a wealth of insights about modern Chinese consumers. This compilation has fascinating perspectives because in addition to research, some of the writers are insiders writing about their own experiences and those of their peers in a given demographic. We see this book as an important reference in this section along with our own observations and experience in the market.

The New Middle Class

China's new middle class is driving consumer spending growth. While the majority of Chinese consumers are not in the affluent or middle-income groups, there is a huge middle class, it's growing and it's expected to reshape China's consumption market. It's expected that the number of middle class families will rise as a result of China's plans to achieve an urbanization rate of over 65% by 2030.

Meanwhile, as coastal areas are already developed and saturated, the urbanization process will expand to western and inland areas. According to McKinsey, the share of the middle class from first tier cities is expected to decrease to from about 40% in 2002 to 22% by 2022 while the middle class in lower tier centers, especially third tier cities, grows.

Another driving force is the implementation of the two-child policy that replaced the one-child policy in 2016. The policy was introduced in the hopes of avoiding the demographic time bomb of an aging population, to boost domestic consumption in the short term and to help balance the working age population in the long run.

This group isn't a direct counterpart to the middle class as understood in the West. Goldman Sachs estimates its size at 146 million using the metric of an average annual income of nearly 12,000 USD or 83,000 RMB. While others, using varying salary thresholds, come up with different numbers, it's clear that it's a large market.

How are they similar to and different from the middle class in the West? The vast majority of them are urbanites who live in highrises rather than suburbanites who live in detached houses. They have enough leisure time and spending power to be able to seriously consider lifestyle choices. They have the means to take vacations, collectively spending $261 billion in 2016 according to the United Nations World Tourism Organization. Goldman Sachs predicts them to be spending $450 billion vacationing overseas by 2025.

They enjoy the ambiance of a coffee shop enough to support over 2,000 Starbucks locations in more than 100 cities, not to mention all of Starbucks' competitors both foreign and domestic. The upper end of the group sent more than 300,000 of their children overseas to school in 2015, contributing $9.8 billion to the US economy alone.

These lives of comfort and choice that were nearly unimaginable 20 years ago, and some of the rapid shifts that have taken place in Chinese society, also mean that traditional and modern ways coexist and family life has more variation than in the past. For example, some of these families have "three generations under one roof", as in the past, while others don't.

They generally spend less than 50% of their income on necessities, and are willing to spend more on life experiences, fine dining, wellness, lifestyle products and affordable luxury products. Products that go on the body or in the body are a focus of intense spending.

"Consumers outside of China have a much different palette in terms of what they are willing to buy online and are less willing to buy online in general. Thus the approach to these markets cannot be so dependent on any one ecosystem, but rather needs to depend on connectivity between different local, regional and global ecosystems."

— Carson McKelvey, Chief Experience Officer, Tofugear

Wealthy "Tuhao"

Attitudes toward wealth changed dramatically as China opened up under Deng. The rich aren't scorned by the Communist party and are seen as key to the country's success and economic prosperity. China has plenty of millionaires and billionaires, although less per capita than many other places.

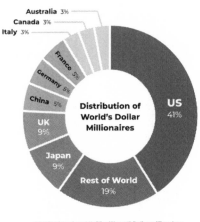

Distribution of world's 33 million US Dollar millionaires
Source: Credit Suisse Global Wealth Report 2016

Tuhao (土豪) roughly translates as "new rich," and is seen as a mildly unflattering. Tuhao includes the people, usually men and usually outside top tier cities, who made vast amounts of money in the early days of opening up in the 1980s and 90s. This was a time when entrepreneurship was new, risky, largely unregulated and still frowned upon by many. No returns were assured at the time and many ventures were highly suspect. Some were also just very lucky. The term has also grown to include purchasing behaviour by ordinary people that is seen as spontaneous.

Real estate investment is a prime source of wealth in China and many in this group used relationships with local governments to buy public assets cheaply and benefitted when China's urbanization drive kicked into high gear. Others lucked into huge payouts from local governments who were redeveloping areas within or near cities. There was little guidance, regulation or oversight so the sums people received varied greatly. Many were cheated and underpaid but others did very well for themselves. Small farmers and property holders suddenly became chaierdai (拆二代), "rich through demolition," a tuhao sub-group. Others established their wealth with businesses and investments, IT, mining, pharmaceuticals, finance, digital industries including online gaming, e-commerce and energy.

Since many tuhao are from poor or working class backgrounds and became suddenly wealthy, they feel a need to broadcast their new status with ostentatious displays that are often seen as tawdry or lacking in sophistication by other elites and younger generations who have grown up with different ideas about fashion and taste. They want the world to see how "luxurious" their lives are. As such, their consumption habits are often criticised or made fun of. However, because of them, China is second only to the US in terms of retail space dedicated to luxury products and, in 2016, China accounted for one third of the world's luxury spending.

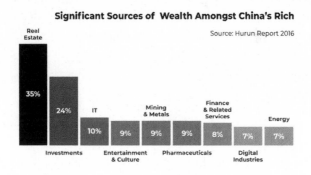

In the past, shows of wealth, such as luxury watches, were used as proxies to demonstrate stability reliability, trust and connections. This was especially so for business owners when dealing with potential partners or local officials within China. They were also seen as portable stores of wealth in case of emergency.

This has changed somewhat in recent years with government policies that were introduced to curb graft and the movement of funds out of the country. Import duties from 30 to 60 per cent were levied and actions were taken against agents making overseas purchases for customers. This has resulted in a shift to antique and pre-owned luxury watches.

There has also been mockery of things tuhao have traditionally spent their money on leading to a preference for goods associated with taste and class, such as red wine, and items that show restraint. This group has also started donating its money and time to good causes. For a nation not known for its charity, this may indicate those that have come from humble roots may not have forgotten them and want to put their money to practical use.

For all these reasons, it's important to consider a luxury customer's background and motivations as well as the current social and regulatory climate in China. It's also important to focus on products that are subtle and low key while still having some that are more vivid and loud. A quote from China's Evolving Consumers sums it up nicely, "China's rich want to be recognized as a class with class."

Maturing Millennials

Chinese millennials, born in the 80s and 90s and now between 20 and 39 years old, are hitting prime consumption age. Described as educated, open-minded and tech-savvy, they make up 31% of China's total population, representing 415 million consumers. BCG estimates that by 2021, millennials will make up 46% of China's urban population. They will experience increasing purchasing power and will gradually become the main consumers of products and services.

Due to the implementation of the one-child policy in 1979, most of them are the only child in their family and had parents and grandparents eager to give them the best of everything. They were the center of the universe. The little prince/princess/emperor factor is strong in this generation, which makes them prioritize their desires instead of their needs.

As a result, when it comes to consumption, they're more demanding and more willing to spend. They want good products and services and they want them fast. They're eager to lead a quality life, instead of merely satisfying their basic needs.

On top of that, Chinese millennials grew up during China's economic reforms and the digital revolution that brought increasing global connectivity. They're far more educated and globally aware than their parents. They love to show their close connection to the rest of the world by buying standout and niche foreign brands. This also demonstrates their one-of-a-kind tastes and distinguishes them from the crowd.

Chinese millennials highly cherish individuality and originality and never hesitate to spend more to get the products and services they want. They are health, wellness and fitness conscious, brand sophisticated and are trading up to premium, luxury, and foreign products in the cosmetics and body care categories.

As they grew up with the internet, they are accustomed to both the real world and virtual worlds. They're far more advanced at e-commerce participation and at integrating tech into everyday life than their Western

"Chinese consumers are almost uniquely enthusiastic about anything on a smartphone. So things are adopted very rapidly. That plus the really large scale makes China a pretty dynamic market with lots of niche players emerging all the time."

— Jeffrey Towson, Managing Partner of Towson Capital and author of The One Hour China Book counterparts. Exploring, purchasing and interacting online are their daily routines. Therefore, it's no surprise that they're savvy online, active social media users and mobile shoppers.

The Younger Generation: Post-00s

The younger generation in China live very different lives from their parents and are caught between saving for large purchases or enjoying life and spending now. Keep in mind that big ticket items, such as real estate or cars, cost much more in China in relation to income. They're willing to spend on their own interests and save money to invest in practicalities and passions in the long-term. They usually don't consume to excess or spend beyond their means. According to Tencent's recent survey, 84% of Post-00s respondents say they wouldn't spend more than they're able to.

"Post 2000s have the opposite shopping habits of their parents. They are less inclined to save their money and spend a larger proportion of their wages. They're particularly fond of trendy products and use online shopping more often. Although they're likely to become more conservative spenders as they establish new families, this group is more willing to spend money than previous generations."

— Zachary Ang,
Regional Business Development Manager, VIP.com

The ease of e-commerce is the magnet pulling this group to do their spending now. The number of online shoppers in China has steadily increased since 2006 reaching 467 million by 2016. In 2015, people aged 10 to 19 made up 24.5% of those shoppers and people aged 20 to 29 made up 31% of the total.

This young generation is more brand conscious, more likely to have engaged in overseas travel and grew up with digital consumption. Alibaba and JD.com have a 75% market share in e-commerce with niche players taking up the rest and those under 28 make up 40% of shoppers on Alibaba's Taobao. They are well-versed in getting discounts and deals and flock to apps and sites that specialize in group buying and other discounts.

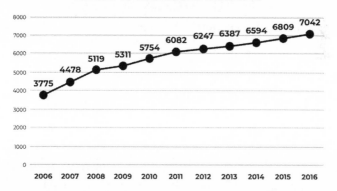

Number of Graduates in Thousands

China turns out tons of fresh graduates every year from local universities and returning from abroad. They're always looking for something new and want to improve their health and skills. Health-related apps, time-saving tips and stress management guides are very popular with this group as are promotions, discounts and group buying.

Since the one-child policy wasn't relaxed until 2016, most of them are only children. As most of their parents are also the only child in their family, this generation is called "second generation only children (独生二代)". As they never had to share their parent's love, attention or resources with siblings and were born in an era of affluence, they're somewhat spoiled.

Having grown up during a time of rapid technological development, they're open to new experiences, respect differences and show a greater ability to adapt than previous generations. They like to express their feelings and views and challenge authority.

This generation is savvy about online influencers and they feel that they can categorize them into trusted sources that they can rely on and those who are just out to make money. As such, social media doesn't seem to have the same influence on their decisions as it does on those older than them. In their opinion, many online promoters are materialistic and money-oriented. They don't think their recommendations are reliable. They're more likely to respect influencers who demonstrate knowledge and expertise, have a background or qualifications related to their online activities or have a primary income source from another profession.

When it comes to the choice between domestic and foreign products, it's worth noting that over 50% of respondents don't consider foreign products better choices. They think domestic products are as good as foreign ones.

Single Young People

Young people in China are increasingly choosing to postpone marriage and childbearing. In 2017, about 15% of China's population were single adults with almost half of them between the ages of 20 and 29. Due to high property prices and the increasing costs of raising a family, many young people are avoiding settling down.

With more disposable income on hand and fewer responsibilities, this group prefers quality products and treating themselves. They spend more money on entertainment and recreation (including e-sports, animation, comics and videos), tourism, personal products, cosmetics, small household appliances and vocational training.

An Alibaba report shows that in recent years, solo use items are gaining traction. Sales of mini-microwaves have increased 970%, mini-washing machine sales have gone up 630% and sales of personal hot pots have increased 200%. Restaurants and food manufacturers are making more options for solo diners and Japanese chain Muji is now making rice cookers, ovens and kettles in smaller sizes.

And they're not afraid to spend. 43% of tier 1 city residents and over 67% of those living in 3rd to 5th tier cities living paycheck to paycheck. In a survey of singles including Beijing, Shanghai and Shenzhen, 31.6% of singles spend most on entertainment or social consumption and 28.6% buy luxury products without hesitating.

Social media influencers and key opinion leaders (KOLs) are important to this group. They want to present an image of looking good on the outside and being good on the inside. This is driving growth in the fitness and athleisure markets. Some in this market estimate that between 30% and 40% of their customer base is single.

This group's companionship needs are expected to boost the pet industry and industries associated with socializing, such as catering and board games. A Sinolink Securities report predicts that convenience stores and delivery services will also become big growth areas for the future.

Young Men

Young male consumers, especially the post-95 generation, have become another consumption force. They care much more about their appearance and personal image than previous generations, so they're willing to spend more on haircare, clothing and fitness. A remarkable increase in male grooming products has been noticed in this consumer group.

The rise in popularity of highly polished young K-pop and C-pop stars has started a trend among young men in China to buy beauty products. The mainland male skincare and cosmetics market is expected to reach 1.9 billion yuan by the end of 2019. Men are adding more products to their routines, they want better products and they want products that are made for men rather than unisex products.

And they do a lot of their shopping online. A survey by China's bankcard association reports that 23% of male consumers spend more than 5,000 RMB a month shopping online. By the end of 2017, 47% of China's online shoppers were male and 65% of the country's cross-border e-commerce shoppers were male. Young men between 18 to 26 in top-tier cities were key drivers of that growth.

White-collar Women

They're career-focused, image conscious, well-rounded individuals living in cities who seize the day while always setting goals and looking ahead. They seek lifestyle products that make them feel confident but aren't ostentatious. They're interested in longevity and holistic health.

Many of these women, though they live in top tier cities now, are from humble backgrounds in smaller cities or rural areas. Their strong competitive drive and perfectionism can sometimes get in the way of healthy personal relationships. They may feel the need to stand out as the highest achiever among their friends and may have impossibly high standards for romantic partners or marriage prospects.

Their need to stand out extends to their clothing and fashion choices. They're willing to spend on quality makeup and unique yet trendy clothes.

They lead workaholic lifestyles and like to dress well. They're willing to change career trajectory and get further education depending on business and industry trends. More and more are willing to start their own businesses as well. They enjoy their careers and the single lifestyle but also face strong internal and family pressure to marry and have children. As a result, they live with anxiety and uncertainty about conflicting roles, expectations, desires, goals and opportunities which change as they get older and enter middle age.

Being subject to these pushes and pulls from different directions, different aspirations and different ideas about how to achieve them means that they shouldn't be addressed as a single monolithic group. On top of that, marketing campaigns aimed at working women that assume they're all the same or aimed at one subgroup may encounter a backlash. As such, it's best to be subtle and embrace the diverse choices women make.

The book China's Evolving Consumers, presents a telling example of how things can go wrong for brands. SKII made an ad featuring single women talking to their mothers. The mothers were regulars at a matchmaking meeting in a park in Shanghai where parents tried to arrange matches for their children. The women talked about their real marriage concerns and worries in the emotional ad. The ad resonated with women who had decided on a more traditional path but flopped with women who have decided to make a go of things on their own. It didn't play well with women see a life forged on their own as exciting rather than pitiable.

Successful single women want their independence, courage and achievements to be admired and showcased and are averse to a view of life that casts them as people who are destined to follow a list of predefined roles and responsibilities that don't reflect their personalities.

Young, Urban Couples

Most in this group were born in the 1980s (Post 80s in China) and 1990s (Post 90s). The older couples in this group are mostly married while the younger ones are mainly in serious relationships or living together. The age for marriage in top tier cities is around 33 years old for men and 30 years old for women. In smaller cities and rural areas, more traditional beliefs persist and women are often married before they're 27 while men usually marry before they're 30.

In the 1980s, people married at around 23 years old for men and 20 for women. The age of marriage has risen for several reasons. There are about 30 million more men than women and long hours devoted to studies and then to careers leave little time to socialize. All that time spent studying and working means women outpace men in terms of education and career achievements, making it more difficult for them to find partners who meet or exceed their expectations. More couples live together before marrying due to greater social acceptance and many in this group are also delaying marriage due to fears of becoming fang nu, or "house slaves" stuck paying off a mortgage for the rest of their working lives.

Ranking	Country	Average age at marriage
1	Germany	33.1
2	Brazil	30.8
3	Japan	30.5
4	United States	27.9
5	United Kingdom	27.9
6	Thailand	26.7
7	Turkey	26.2
8	Russia	25.7
9	Philippines	25.6
10	China	25.3

All the same, there's enormous family and social pressure to marry leading some to make poor decisions that have seen the divorce rate rise 63% in the last ten years.

Their strong belief in education as a means of advancement and self-development has come from their parents and they will transmit it to their children. A favourite pastime for couples with children is finding and investing, mostly online, in safe products, educational toys and classes for their young ones. While some young couples enjoy ostentatious items that show off their status, others prefer a low key approach and prefer to save money or spend it on health supplements, fresh fruit, sporting goods, quality skincare, travel opportunities and red wine. They're also strong consumers of services, including travel, hospitality, healthcare, entertainment and personal care.

Among these couples are those who've come to live in cities from more rural areas. In some of these places, the one child policy was enforced less strictly so some of them have brothers and sisters although for a majority, their children will never have aunts, uncles or cousins. If their parents were granted properties by the state and have been lucky with investments, they can help their children with down payments, childcare and will also pass on their wealth to only one child, enabling them to have a good start in their adult life.

Young urban couples are all involved with a third party — their mobile phones. The Post- 90s generation are digital natives and those born in the 80s came of age with the internet and have been avid users ever since. These groups are early adopters, novelty seekers, constant users making up 54% of all internet users in China and have particularly embraced the mobile internet. For many, lacking brothers, sisters, cousins and other extended family bonded them even more strongly to their phones. It has transformed the way they take watch entertainment, get information do their shopping and interact socially.

In 2017, there were 81 million paid online video users in the mainland, most of them taking in that content on their phones throughout the day as they work and get news and information from friends, websites, newsletters updates and more.

They can shop wherever they are and at any time. Highly integrated social media, online markets and mobile payment systems have made China the world's largest e-commerce market. In 2016, the National Bureau of Statistics reported that retail sales online had reached $745 billion USD which was an increase of 26.2% from the previous year. Online sales make up 15.5% of the total retail of $4.7 trillion USD.

Most young couples without children treat their homes as a place to sleep and sometimes eat with their social life and most meals taken outside the home. This is ironic given what a financial burden an apartment is for these young couples. In lower tier cities, there's less pressure and more free time but also lower wages and a more subdued lifestyle. This creates a dilemma for some young couples with those from lower tier cities yearning for the wages and opportunities of larger cities while a micro trend has begun among couples from larger centres who are moving to smaller cities in search of more free time and less stress.

One key trend to be aware of with this group is premiumization. With most of their money going toward mortgages, young couples can be very value oriented or very focused on high quality, depending on the product concerned. For example, young couples have a strong preference for premium imported baby milk powder. Other products that have been predicted by Kantar to benefit from this trend are yogurt, biscuits, skincare, makeup and personal care products.

Young Mothers

Young mothers in China are often caught between tradition and modernity. They're caught between a new life they're building for themselves and their child, two sets of parents and grandparents from another generation. Grandparents in China often play a much more active and vocal role in the lives of their grandchildren. This can even mean debating the child's parents over which specific brands to buy or even what to feed their children. This can be further complicated by brands that, knowing the strong role grandparents can play, have created their advertising messages specifically to sway this older generation.

The path mothers choose to navigate this minefield is respectful yet passive. They listen, look after their parents' health and buy them supplements while ignoring negative comments, tucking away gifted items they don't like at the back of drawers and venting to other mothers outside of the family. The products mothers choose also provide a way for them to be distinct from their own parents and to establish their new identity as mothers. They allow mothers to introduce new routines that help them, placate their child while avoiding upsetting their parents. They're also busy trying to keep up with the Joneses and many of their decisions are highly influenced by what they see other young parents doing.

While they respect their parents, mothers tend to disregard their advice as from another era. They seek advice in person and online from other mothers who they trust and do a lot of other research before making purchasing decisions. They're very cautious and aware of health and safety issues.

This focus on health can be seen in the kitchen. Modern ovens, cookware, juicers, blenders and yoghurt makers are hallmarks of this focus on health. The family eats out less and fresh food, imported items and organic food are staples.

These outlays, as well as extra costs for children's clothing and pre-school, help young mothers build their identity as mothers and part of the middle class, but they also put financial pressure on families. Even with good salaries, couples can feel like they're on a treadmill trying to keep up with expenses. They feel financially fragile.

Mothers also spend on themselves with beauty remaining a priority. Gym memberships are seen as a necessity if not to attend classes then to demonstrate a commitment to health and fitness and keep up with their peers.

Motherhood is seen by young mothers as a transformative role. It has helped them to learn and grow and become strong, enabled them to bond with a new community of women, mostly online and has helped them to navigate new roles within their extended families. Their consumption and online engagement has played a large role in this.

Senior Citizens

Instead of staying home and looking after their grandchildren, modern seniors are more willing to pursue a lavish lifestyle than previous generations. They're cultivating their own interests and travelling. Meanwhile, health products and medical services are also in strong demand with this group.

Today's seniors have saved with a view to enjoying their retirement and many have saved a hefty portion of their money over China's economic growth years and have sizeable nest eggs. They have enough to contribute to the educations of their children and grandchildren, spend on themselves and pass wealth on to the next generation.

The retirement age is around 55 for women and 60 for men. Still active, seniors take up hobbies and sports in greater numbers, learning to play instruments, dancing, doing tai chi, joining groups of all kinds, hiking and traveling. They can be seen in city parks in the early morning exercising or dancing in groups.

While those born before 1960 hold more tightly to their purse strings, for those born after 1960, although they have conservative tastes and tend to cook at home, they're not afraid to occasionally spend money on travel and are taking their chance to see the world. They don't see their savings as emergency funds any more.

However, travelling abroad is so new to them, other countries are so unknown to them and foreign languages are so unfamiliar to them that they tend to travel in groups. They trust group tour organizers to know the best places to stay, the most interesting sights and local specialties to eat but they prefer small groups that allow some freedom, show authentic local life and don't make them stand out as they travel. Older travellers feel that they need guides to bridge language and cultural barriers.

Seniors are also interested in maintaining their health. Vitamin and mineral supplements are a common gift to older members of the family. Health foods and reasonably priced fitness classes aimed at their age group would suit many older Chinese people.

Elder care facilities are also a focus from investment from within China as well as by global firms. Traditional state care centres have rooms that are shared by up to 7 people. This isn't where China's middle class elderly want to spend their later years. They want to be in places that allow recreation and socializing and have organized events for them to take part in. As this generation of elderly is used to smartphones, integrated digital solutions could be used to connect them to other seniors and to their families.

Mobile Digital First

No matter the age or income group, Chinese people use mobile digital solutions all the time. Because of the wide range of mobile digital solutions available there, many daily tasks are accomplished on one's phone. On top of that, its huge population means that it has the largest group of internet users in the world, estimated by the China Internet Network Information Center (CNNIC) at over 800 million in 2018 with 98.% accessing the internet via mobile devices.

Chinese consumers depend more and more on their phones and the internet for social networking, news, entertainment and shopping. They also do a variety of daily errands and tasks, like paying for public transportation, sharing work-related files, ordering food and delivering online purchases, with multi-functional apps like WeChat. According to Nielsen, nearly 60% of Chinese consumers spend over two hours on their smartphones every day, while 14% spend more than five hours.

In tandem with this, e-commerce has grown rapidly in China. Statistics from CNNIC show that by June, 2018, the number of online shoppers in China reached 569 million, and that of online mobile shoppers reached 557 million. In other words, over 70% of Chinese people who have access to the internet have made online purchases.

Moreover, according to the National Bureau of Statistics, e-commerce is a new driving force in China's retail industry with online retail sales reaching over 4 trillion RMB (590 billion USD) in the first half of 2018 with year-on-year growth of 30.1%. China is the top online retail market in the world, and it's the absolute leader in digital consumption by population size and market scale.

The explosion of e-commerce in China can also be attributed to all the services backed by online sales channels, digital payment tools and express delivery services. With a variety of e-commerce platforms available, users only need to download an app to check out products anytime, anywhere. Express delivery service providers are also widespread and reliable with logistics information that can be viewed and tracked easily via apps. It's like having a mall in your pocket.

The two most used mobile payment tools in China are Alipay, originally developed by Alibaba and now operated by Ant Financial, and WeChat Pay, developed by Tencent. Their speed and reliability are key contributors to the popularity of online shopping in China. They can also be used offline in brick-and-mortar stores and making payments by scanning with smartphones is seen as normal in China. Statistics from the CNNIC show that the number of mobile payment users had reached 566 million by June, 2018.

The internet has also made foreign products more accessible through cross-border e-commerce platforms. Young adults between 18 and 35 are the biggest cross-border shoppers. The most up to date estimate of cross-border transaction volume is from iiMedia in 2017 which predicted the total for 2018 to hit 9 trillion RMB (1.3 trillion USD).

Social Media and Social Commerce

China has social media mania. Nearly everyone in China, young, old and of all socio-economic levels, is active on social media. Statistics from WeAreSocial show that, by January 2018, the number of active social media users in China had reached is in the hundreds of millions and has a very high penetration rate. The average daily time spent on social media, via any device ,is about 2 hours.

WeChat (Weixin) and Weibo are the most popular social media platforms in China. WeChat has a Chinese version, called Weixin, and an international version and it now has over 1 billion registered users all over the world.

The number of Weibo monthly active users reached 431 million in June, 2018. For Chinese people, social media is not only a tool that they use to receive the latest news and connect with friends and other like-minded people, but also a place where they can enjoy all kinds of entertainment, go shopping and do their daily errands.

On social media, people share their experiences and their purchases. As their connections are close family, friends and trusted sources, especially on WeChat, they're more likely to trust their comments and recommendations.

People considering buying a new item also go through comments and feedback on social media as part of their decision-making process before they buy. Concerns about fake positive feedback on e-commerce platforms are widespread so people look to key opinion leaders and influencers on social media for more reliable feedback. And they're not just looking for product reviews, they're also looking for ideas about what to buy.

As a result, social media has become a battlefield for brands. They offer discounts, launch campaigns, create ads and invite celebrities and credible bloggers to create word-of-mouth posts in order to reach their potential customers.

Chinese consumers can now finish the whole purchasing process from research and selection to final transaction on social media, or even within one app. This convenience has caused them to rely on social media more and more for their online shopping needs and has made social media a major sales channel.

This is how and why social media is so closely connected with e-commerce in China.

CHAPTER 9

4 Changing Roles You Need to Understand

New retail has and will continue to radically change customer behavior and company strategies. Trend-sensitive brands have already realized that consumers need to be at the center, not just in terms of the final purchasing transaction, but also production, delivery and promotion. The old role of product purchaser is being replaced by new roles as co-producer and mini-influencer as people take an active role in the creation of their products and the marketing efforts surrounding them.

While these roles have already been shifting online for some time, we'll continue to see this transformation occur in more sophisticated and embedded ways offline. Brands and merchants that want to do well as these changes take hold understand that the control now lies with consumers and they need to play on their terms. This chapter is about this transformation as it's taking place in China.

1 From Brick and Mortar Store to Data Collection Site

Previously, when companies wanted to cut costs, they closed stores and relocated goods and services online. With the emergence of big data, market players have realized that brick and mortar stores are more than just retail outlets. They're data collection sites.

> "More personalized communications and products necessitate a strong customer relationship management system that captures relevant data and turns it into something meaningful for the consumer. How to do this empathetically and with purpose will determine how brands in high-competition, low differentiation categories stay relevant to consumers."
>
> — Michael Norris,
> Research and Strategy Manager, AgencyChina

Alibaba is continuing to invest in brick-and-mortar retailing to test algorithms and collect data about customers, products and shopping behaviour. Companies can build databases covering membership, purchasing activity and customer preferences and adjust product offerings in real time. They can also design creative marketing campaigns with a higher rate of audience engagement.

A good illustration of this process is Chinese department store chain Intime which has taken on a digital transformation since joining forces with Alibaba in 2014. There are 62 Intime store in 33 cities, where customers can use the company's mobile app, Miaojie, to exercise membership privileges, scan products to get information, find their way around the stores or get product recommendations and discounts. When consumers aren't in the store, the app notifies them about new products, discounts and promotional events based on their preferences.

The department store chain also revamped their supply chain behind the scenes to facilitate multiple purchase, collection and delivery options.

The app helps detect the closest Intime store and, in major cities, can make customer deliveries within 2 hours. The department store was also the first in China to use Alipay as a payment option.

Intime was also the first department store in China to offer fully digitized paid memberships. Members of its INTIME365 plan receive access to exclusive service and promotions for 365 RMB ($54 USD) per year. They just need to link their account with their Alibaba membership and the system offers personalised service based on their account history.

Alibaba's first Tao Café was launched in 2017 in Hangzhou. It's a cashier-less cafe, that only requires a smartphone to enter and make a purchase using Alibaba's Taobao app. Purchases are tracked using facial and voice recognition systems and bills are automatically generated bills when customers pass through the store's gate.

Alibaba can place itself at the center of the shopping cycle by using data to create an optimal product mix and spot new consumption trends as they emerge. Cameras in the store detect hot spots and hot shelves, which in turn affects future store designs. Alibaba simplifies purchases for consumers while gathering data.

Case Study

A New Generation of Mom and Pop Stores

Despite the fact that China has the biggest e-commerce market in the world, there are still thousands of mom and pop shops in rural areas which haven't been digitised. Alibaba's management platform Ling Shou Tong ("retail-integrated" in English) is aimed at these shops to help owners to do better inventory management of their stores. Owners get access to advanced customer data, analytics, warehousing and logistics systems, while the tech giant uses the stores as fulfillment-and-delivery centers.

> *"Nationwide logistics and on-demand delivery are critical capabilities that enable almost everything else and Chinese consumers aren't willing to wait very long. This infrastructure and service is much harder to replicate than web pages and online capabilities."*
>
> — Jeffrey Towson, Managing Partner of Towson Capital and author of The One Hour China Book

2 From Consumer to Content Creator and Co-producer

In the New Retail era, producers and consumers are no longer isolated and separate. The two roles are interrelated and there are more and more cases of brands collaborating with consumers to make their own personally tailored products and consumers volunteering to promote products that impress them. The average consumer has evolved into a prosumer who helps to design and produce products and the business model is no longer B2C (business to consumer) but C2B (consumer to business).

This shift has been accelerated in China because of the fast pace of digital change and the wide adoption of new technologies. It's created a market where retailers have to adopt big data analytics to deal with this transformation or be left behind.

A simple example from July 2019, a DIY Selfie bottle from Coke, shows this relationship well. In Macau, the company released six special edition cans featuring iconic tourist spots in Macau. Fans who spent more than MOP 500 at The Venetian and purchased one of the special cans could take a selfie at their special booth and receive a 500ml personalized Coca-Cola bottle with their selfie on it.

Another way that consumers will increasingly take over marketing roles is shown in how brands leverage the fan effect. A recent campaign from L'Oréal Paris Skincare is a good example.

Traditionally, the company's ambassadors were mature, established celebrities like Gong Li and Yuchun Li. As part of a new approach to ramp up sales during China's big e-commerce festivals, they've signed several up-and-coming idols as "Best Friends of the Brand".

One of their new signees is 20 year old rising star, Xukun Cai. He came to fame as the champion in an American Idol-style reality show called Idol Producer. He's a rapper, singer and songwriter and has almost 22 million followers on Weibo.

His credentials as an influencer for the brand were cemented during JD.com's 618 Festival when the product he had endorsed, Youth Code Pre-essence, was a top seller. Cai's fans, excited to see him being appreciated by a high-prestige fashion brand, wanted to help him maintain this relationship by reposting L'Oréal content and making CGC featuring L'Oréal products. Their efforts led to Youth Code Pre-essence making the Weibo hot topic list, the equivalent of Twitter's trending list.

However, conversion based on fan admiration can't last long since Cai's fans are loyal to him rather than the brand. If Cai was hired by another brand or L'Oréal stopped their partnership with him, his fans would likely follow him and might even turn on L'Oréal in retaliation for the company stopping their association with him.

Another part of this shift involves cultivating specific fan bases. Tencent announced at its UP 2018 Summit that it's going to focus on fandoms in the categories of movies, games, traditional Chinese culture, animation and more. Unlike the tentative collaborations between fashion brands and idols, Tencent will integrate content related to these fandoms into its products with a focus on games. The hope is to develop its own IP franchises as a result. These giant fan bases will likely be the future battlefield that media companies compete for. Alibaba also announced an IP incubation plan, known as Big Entertainment (Da Wen Yu / 大文娱), in 2016.

3   From Tech Company to Financial Institution

The two main players in China, Tencent and Alibaba, began as tech companies but they've gone on to develop financial tools that have become so widespread and indispensable that they've taken on many of the functions of traditional financial institutions.

Launched in 2004, Alipay was first used as an escrow service to enable secure transactions on Alibaba's Taobao website. (Taobao is an online market for small businesses, similar to eBay.) Alipay later expanded to a full-fledged online and offline payment system that could be used by any merchant. It was spun off in 2010 and is now under the management of Alibaba affiliate, Ant Financial. Alipay was one of the earliest online payment systems in the world and gained an enormous foothold because it had no transaction fees, it was reliable and Alibaba's online platforms had huge user bases.

In 2014, WeChat launched its own payment system for peer-to-peer (P2P) transfers and in-app purchases. It too has grown beyond its initial scope and is now used to do all kinds of transactions online and offline. It's used by hundreds of millions of people and also doesn't charge transaction fees.

Both companies are on the forefront of China's drive to increase cashless payments across the nation and have forged partnerships with banks and offline merchants to accomplish this aim.

Despite of the fact that Alipay was the first to enter the market, more and more experts predict that WeChat Pay may take the number one spot eventually. The payment services are used in different ways. Alipay is used on the hugely popular Taobao site and is usually used for big ticket items. WeChat Pay is used more for daily errands, purchases within WeChat, which can include tickets for train journeys or flights, and paying friends. Because they don't charge transaction fees, both payment methods can be used frequently and for small amounts without worry.

In terms of use by individuals outside of China, both payment solutions had previously only been available to those with registered bank accounts in China. However, WeChat Pay announced in late 2018 that certain foreign credit card holders would be able to use its internal China payment services. This applies to foreigners residing in Hong Kong, Macau or Taiwan using credit cards issued by Visa, Mastercard or Japanese issuer JCB. The app will make currency exchanges automatically.

For merchants outside of China, third parties enable both payment systems to be set up within their stores to facilitate commerce with Chinese tourists. Alipay is accepted in 26 countries across Europe, North America, East Asia and Southeast Asia and WeChat Pay can handle payments in 12 currencies in 15 countries and regions.

"What I can say is that certainly in Asia, we are seeing this new digital economy grow and develop. China is leading the charge but equally, we see a big market in ASEAN as well. China has around 5.6 trillion USD in retail and ASEAN has 2 trillion but those markets continue to grow whether they're Chinese or Asian."

— Anson Bailey, Partner, Business Development at
KPMG China

In addition to offering an increasing array of financial services, including investment services, insurance, online banking and social credit ratings services, Tencent and Alibaba have large teams of in-house bankers with many from well-known American investment banks such as Goldman Sachs. They've also backed a large proportion of China's billion-dollar privately held unicorns and are behind some of the country's biggest stock market listings.

4   Brands are Retailers, Retailers are Brands

New Retail will be based on long-term relationships with customers. It's the story of unforgettable and inspiring experiences. Brands, retailers and manufacturers have realized that they need to design a distribution process that centers around the consumer, instead of their individual agendas.

If companies don't understand these new relationships, it will cost them in the end. If they do, even simple initiatives can reap huge rewards.

CHAPTER 10

It's More Than Shopping

When Jack Ma coined the term New Retail in 2016, he was announcing Alibaba's goal to combine offline and online retail and logistics into one dynamic and tech-driven whole. There was no question that companies and brands were eager to find the new ways to reach Chinese consumers, who have the highest rate of mobile shopping in the world. By 2021, eMarketer predicts that 79.3% of Chinese shoppers will be paying via their mobiles versus 30% of Americans and 22% of Germans.

But New Retail isn't just about shopping and in this chapter we'll explore its effects on other market players.

It's no longer enough just to understand a customer's needs, it's become essential to provide unforgettable experiences. As a result, entire industries are shifting from a transactional approach to relational and experimental mindsets. Artificial intelligence (AI), augmented reality (AR), virtual reality (VR) the internet of things (IoT), the blockchain, live-streaming and many, many other technologies allow brands to be more sensitive to their customers and to adjust to them in real time.

In 2016 Jack Ma predicted that new technologies and innovations would swiftly emerge in all spheres of our life around the globe and by 2019, New Retail's infrastructure has been firmly established in China. More and more companies are now focusing on consumer-centric innovation, cashier-free technologies, mobile services and AR/VR technologies. This requires a high level of collaboration between all participants and Chinese consumers are getting used to being co-producers and co-creators of their favourite products and services. Tech - driven New Retail is the new reality in China.

1 Online Merge Offline (OMO) Grocery Stores

New mobile apps became an opportunity for companies to engage with consumers directly in real time. There are several OMO grocery stores which have already successfully implemented mobile services in their business model.

Freshippo Supermarkets (Formerly Hema)

In 2018 with Freshippo supermarkets, Alibaba implemented its new vision of grocery stores in China. As of 2019 there are over 100 stores across the country. Some stores in Beijing and Shanghai provide 24-hour delivery service. The secret of its overwhelming success is that Freshippo provides customers with more than shopping. It's also a fresh food restaurant and people can buy fresh groceries and seafood and have it delivered to their home, have it cooked and eat it in-store or have it cooked and delivered to their home.

Super Species

In December 2018, Tencent bought a stake in Super Species, a fresh food supermarket, cooked food outlet and high-end goods retailer, from one of China's largest supermarket chain operators, Yonghui Superstores. The stores operate in a similar fashion to Freshippo so the partnership allows Tencent to compete with Alibaba on the smart supermarket front.

The stores are also known for their unique drone deliveries. EHang UAVs has partnered with the company to do aerial food deliveries for orders within a 4.5 km radius. The drones operate automatically using a networked system and have reduced delivery times from 30 to 15 minutes.

7Fresh

JD.com's Boundaryless Retail can be seen in its 7Fresh supermarkets. Big data analytics and AI used in the stores helps JD not just sell their products but also educate visitors. Smart displays automatically show shoppers where a product is from and its nutritional value. There are also the smart carts that can guide shoppers around the store based on the personal preferences. Their plan is to open 1,000 of these supermarkets in the next three to five years

2 Services and Amenities

Banking

In 2018, China Construction Bank (CCB) opened a bank branch in Shanghai operated by robots with the help of facial recognition, artificial intelligence and virtual reality. Clients can open accounts, transfer money, change currencies, make gold investments and buy wealth management products from a friendly-looking robot. People are also on hand to help and there's a private room available to talk to customer relationship managers via video link.

Banks are also continuing a transition to using more smart machines at branches that can do transactions more complex than basic withdrawals, deposits and bill payments.

Parking

China Mobile and DTMobile have initiated two separate smart parking pilots in in Yunnan and Southeast Guizhou using Narrowband Internet of Things (NB-IoT) connectivity. (NB-IoT is used for low cost connections requiring indoor coverage while maintaining long battery life and high connection density. NB-IoT uses a single narrow-band of 200kHz.)

The system makes it easier for drivers to find free parking spots. This lets cities better manage their paid parking revenue, traffic congestion and pollution. The system can detect parking spots, recognize license plates, guide drivers and take mobile payments.

Auto Vending Machines

Car vending machines in China allow prospective car buyers to book cars for test drives and later purchase. In 2018, in Guangzhou, Alibaba Group, in cooperation with the Ford, installed a car vending machine. It's a tall tower with an elevator like the ones in vertical parking garages. Customers got a chance to choose a car through the app, freely test it for three days and then decide if they want to buy it or not.

Smart Gyms

The touch of New Retail is also visible in modern Chinese gyms. The new generation of sport centers feature small rooms of around 100 square meters. Members spend only 20 minutes doing various exercises in special fitness clothing that's hooked up to monitoring equipment. This new model promises to deliver the same results as the average 2 hour workout in a traditional gym. Members make appointments via WeChat mini program or through the gym's official app. They can also make appointments to meet with personal trainers and coaches. The rooms are available 24/7 with no full-time staff.

Sports

In November 2018 modern technologies were used during the Hangzhou International Marathon. Facial recognition helped organisers prevent cheating. Alibaba's sports affiliate, Alisports was one of the main sponsors and it used its fitness app Ledongli developed special game that used the marathon route as background and included 20 challenges related to

Hangzhou.

Unmanned Laundries

Automats aren't new but in November 2017, Taidi (Teddy) opened the first unmanned laundry featuring a "24-hour care ATM". It offered ATM and internet services as well as automatic hangers. Customers could also have their laundry delivered along with any other deliveries that they'd ordered.

Bathrooms

"Magic Mirrors" using AR and RFID technologies allow women to experiment with their makeup and show what different products look like and then purchase them from the bathroom's vending machine.

3 Healthcare

In 2018, Alibaba Group and Tencent have started optimizing day-to-day medical services and health product delivery.

On Taobao, patients can search for health products, such as supplements, ointments and over-the-counter medicine. Delivery takes 30 minutes during the day and 1 hour at night. Alibaba currently provides this service only in Hangzhou, but in the near future, there will be widespread changes as new technologies are applied. It also offers online consultations with a doctor through Alibaba Health Information Technology (AliHealth), the company's health care flagship.

Tencent's medical unit Doctorwork, is working closely with Shanghai-based startup Trusted Doctors to provide online medical consultations. It offers an ecosystem of online and offline services and uses AI and big data capabilities in partnership with hospitals and clinics across the country to develop healthcare solutions and it's likely that this partnership will also result in access to online medical consultations.

In 2018, China announced the first successful use of a robot dentist to surgically fit a 3D printed implant in the presence of qualified medical staff. This initiative was started because of a lack of qualified dentists in the country and to improve local services.

China's first smart hospital also recently opened in Guangzhou. An AI driven-system provides recommendations and directions to patients before they arrive at the hospital and helps them make appointments. Payments can be made through WeChat accounts and medical profiles can also be accessed by patients through WeChat's facial recognition systems.

AI also helps the doctors as a smart diagnosis system helps doctors diagnose patients and prescribe medications. It's estimated that it reduces examination time by 50% and can diagnose 90% of illnesses that are commonly presented.

In December 2017, The Ministry of Industry and Information Technology (MIIT) of China released a three-year action plan that set specific tech targets for healthcare. The plan's target for AI systems by 2020 was to be able to diagnose more than 95% of common diseases with a false negative rate of less than 1% and the false positive rate of less than 5%. The plan also envisioned the widespread use of AI-enabled service robots to help seniors and children by 2020.

4 Education

It's thought that the same kind of AI and technology that is transforming shopping and consumer experiences will also transform education.

In his book AI Superpowers, Kai-Fu Lee foresees education systems that use technology to tailor more personalized teaching and learning processes. He envisions education systems where a student's digital profile contains detailed records of which concepts they understand well, which concepts they are struggling with, how attentive they are, how quickly they answer questions and more.

He also thinks that teaching will increasingly be done remotely via video links and broadcasts in class. Teachers will be able to gauge understanding through the use of handheld devices that students use to answer questions and do coursework, giving teachers and parents a detailed picture of each student's learning and giving students instant feedback on their progress.

This kind of personalization may lead to classrooms where algorithms assign higher level work to some students and lower level work or extra practice to others. Systems are already in place that help teachers with corrections and tracking student work and he feels in the future, these will become even more common.

Systems may also be used to monitor students and filter for teachers who are more effective at communicating concepts and keeping children engaged.

5 Fun, Convenient, Automated Leisure

Restaurants and Cafes

In 2017, Alibaba first introduced its cashier-less coffee shop, Tao Café, in Hangzhou. The 200 square meter space is fully digitalized. Customers scan the shop's QR code with their Taobao app and use facial recognition to check in. When their order is done, customers see their face and waiting time on the shop's screen. It's a showcase automated environment.

In June, 2018, Western bakery Wedome launched its first unmanned smart bakery. Consumers can pre-order through an app and then pick up their order in the store or use image capture cash registers that recognize the items customers are buying. Visitors can also pre-order by scanning QR codes in menus and collect their orders later from special lockers. Payments are automatically made through their Alipay account.

Museums

Chinese museums now use incredible technology to educate visitors interactively. In May, 2018, the Palace Museum in Beijing organized a high tech interactive exhibition centring on the ancient Chinese painting Along the River During the Qingming Festival. It's a complex scene of holiday celebrations painted on a more than 5 metre long scroll. Visitors got a chance to see the Song dynasty painting in motion with the help of multimedia technology giving them an unforgettable experience of the life of the past.

Cashier-less Karaoke Booths

Chinese consumers can now enjoy their favorite activity, karaoke or KTV, in subway stations. Unmanned mini-booths with karaoke equipment can be used by travellers while they wait for friends or as they make their way home from work. Previously, this was something city dwellers usually did in big groups but that's not necessary with these small rooms that can be accessed by scanning a QR code. Payment is automatically made based on the number of songs or time spent in the booth.

Hair Salons

In August 2015, a new type of hair salon opened in Shenzhen. It became the model for internet salons in China. Appointments and payment are all done via WeChat. There's no hard sell, only hair-cutting. At the end of 2017, the number of active users exceeded 1 million. As of September 12, 2018, there were 298 stores in the city, including 202 in Shenzhen, 77 in Guangzhou, 7 in Foshan, 3 in Shanghai and 9 in Wuhan.

Hotels

In November, 2018, Alibaba opened its first hotel of the future. Alibaba FlyZoo is located in Alibaba's Xixi Park. A robot receptionist, with the help of facial recognition technology, checks guests in, remembers them and puts their data into the system. Robots accompany guests during their stay and the hotel is also equipped with an AI management system allowing guests to control indoor temperatures, lighting, curtains and the TV. Guests can also order room service or buy groceries from nearby stores.

Digital Living

Technology is becoming embedded in all our lives in more and more ways. There will also be more digital links between various areas of our lives. Our online shopping data may begin to influence our eligibility for loans. Our school records might be sent by the click of a button to the universities we're applying to instead of requiring us to fill out forms online or offline. Algorithms will automatically determine if we've achieved the required benchmarks to be granted entry or we could merely scan a code to get a travel visa.

It will make our lives easier and more convenient in many regards but it's important to remember that it will also complicate them in ways that are difficult for many of us to see now.

PART III

The New Retail Live: What's Ahead

CHAPTER 11

How to Win in China's New Retail World and Lessons to Take Home

Since Jack Ma introduced the term New Retail in 2016, there have been significant changes to the retail landscape in China. Market players have quickly realized that a new customer-centric era has emerged. In order to stay competitive, traditional retailers need to delight consumers while building highly integrated supply chains behind the scenes.

In this chapter you'll learn how key Chinese players are optimizing the customer experience, what challenges traditional retailers face and what international brands need to do to stay on their feet in this battlefield.

New Retail at Its Core

Experience versus Product

New Retail has blurred the boundaries between online and offline, retailer and manufacturer, consumer and creator. This new seamless, unified model provides new opportunities to drive recognition and sales.

Previously, brands competed on product alone but now, the game is won by those who provide unforgettable shopping and life experiences.

Smart Digitisation and Automation

Another challenge is implementing innovative and practical digitisation and automation. Big data, AI, machine learning, RFID technology, the blockchain and many other technologies can help retailers to gain insights, track processes and serve customers more flexibly while consumers get faster, more efficient, fun service.

Customized and Personalized Service

Consumer behaviour and preferences are in constant flux. Successful brands need to move fast and provide well-targeted, interesting services together with their products.

China's e-commerce shopping festivals used to attract large numbers of new consumers which was useful for increasing brand awareness, but consumers are much more savvy now and have participated in multiple festivals so they aren't as surprised by brand collaborations with KOLs or the variety of products promoted in offline stores.

Chinese consumers, more than any others in the world, are willing to share massive amounts of data about their identity and preferences but with this come high expectations for personalized experiences. On top of that, personalization, rapid delivery, product satisfaction and good customer service are important factors in terms of brand loyalty. Expectations and pressures on brands to work 24/7 to personalize, customize, and keep up a dialogue with each consumer are increasing.

Shared resources

Higher expectations and increased pressure on retailers is pushing big and small players to optimize processes and increase their capabilities by partnering or sharing resources with Alibaba or Tencent.

How to Win at China's New Retail as a Foreign Brand

Online integration

For many China observers, it might seem like traditional retail models are dead and the whole industry has already made the shift to the New Retail model. In reality, there are still challenges even for Chinese brands and the gap between them and Western companies is not that big. The right business model and approach still allows foreign brands to be competitive.

The good news for Western companies, which are already in China, is that brick-and-mortar stores are not dead. However, to stay on top, you have to enhance your existing retail model by integrating with Chinese digital giants and plugging into their ecosystem, their mobile payment systems and give your customers a reason to talk about your stores and products on social media. Then, optimize your brick-and-mortar stores to collect customer data.

The Chinese market is huge and international newcomers still have an opportunity to get their piece of the pie but social media is crucial. An overwhelming majority of Chinese online users have a social media account and use a variety of apps and platforms. They also operate mostly by mobile. This gives newcomers a chance to start small and test their products on social media before big-scale launches. Whereas even a few years ago your choices for digital engagement were Alibaba and JD.com, now there are numerous marketplaces, platforms, and apps that make it possible. There are solutions for companies of all sizes, means, and risk tolerance.

Alibaba's Tmall Global was the first and is currently the largest cross border marketplace. Foreign brands and retailers build a digital store on the marketplace and place inventory in a bonded warehouse in a free trade zone where products are picked, packed and shipped through

Cainiao. JD.com also has a cross-border commerce marketplace called JD Worldwide and the business model for international brands is virtually the same.

There's also a fairly new cross-border marketplace called Kaola. The company was created by China's technology giant Netease and the platform, by volume of purchases, is China's largest cross-border marketplace. Despite that lofty achievement, few outside China know Kaola because they keep a low profile. Their model is wholesale to retail. They buy products from brands, take possession of inventory and then market, merchandise, sell and fulfill. To date the company has relied primarily on buying from brand's local or overseas distributors. This plays into their focus on offering mass market goods at rock bottom prices.

They found a niche in the cross-border market. Having control of consumer data for customization is a major competitive advantage for the company. Previously, one disadvantage for them was that they had few direct relationships with brands but they are solving this by hiring people in the United States, Europe and elsewhere to develop new business.

Working with Influencers (KOLs)

Finding your target audience and understanding the mindset and preferences of Chinese consumers is the key to success in China. Traditional marketing and ads are not as effective as they used to be. Word of mouth marketing, via social media, is the most efficient strategy in China.

Around half of consumers in China consider shopping a highly social activity and many consumers there belong to online communities where people with common interests share opinions about products.

Social media also serves as a search engine. Recommendations and shopping experiences that people want to talk about play increasingly important roles in the retail process. Many online consumers in China seem to trust other consumers' comments and recommendations. Because of this, and the fact that people in China spend a lot of time online, brands cooperate with key opinion leaders (KOLs) to promote their products and drive sales.

KOL campaigns successfully attract public attention to new brands and products and create positive word of mouth. Here it's important to understand that today's consumers are very experienced and are sensitive to whether a KOL's promotions match their authentic persona or if they feel like ill-fitting cash grabs.

Technology Partnerships

The time to go it alone is gone. In the next few years, we'll see the growth of partnerships and collaborations between retailers and technology players. Don't buy or build technologies by yourself. Find niche companies and create something together or plug into an existing ecosystem.

In China, platforms have existed for some time that allow retailers to access everything from smart logistics, fast delivery solutions and marketing to detailed customer data and full-fledged e-commerce. Alibaba and JD.com both offer these kinds of services. As Ella Kidron, from JD.com puts it, the company "has a vast amount of insight into consumer behavior and consumer preferences. We open up these resources to our brand partners. In addition, through our strategic partnerships, in particular our partnership with Tencent, brands have access to a range of marketing resources."

This stands in marked contrast to a platform like Amazon which retains its data and insights for internal use only and, in recent years, has used these insights to launch their own inhouse brands to compete with brands hosted on its platform.

> *"Alibaba is developing new retail models that are transforming many retail experiences from the grocery story, the car dealership, the local convenience store and even the shopping mall. We are working with our brand partners to incubate the technology, so it can be leveraged by the entire retail industry."*
>
> — Erica Matthews, Head of Corporate Relations, Alibaba Group

Innovative Internal Education

One of the most important keys to success in China is innovative education within your company. Create a culture of innovation and encourage your team to constantly learn and adopt new technology when appropriate. Bring department heads to China and arrange immersive training for them. Help familiarize them with cutting edge digital projects and technologies there and show how they work on the ground and in real life. Without this fundamental shift, New Retail is not possible.

Companies who are willing to use new business models, localize products and make the appropriate operational shifts will see their prospects in China improve quickly and dramatically.

Case Study: Mondelez

For the last ten years, two of the biggest challenges brands have had in making the most of their China business have been localizing products for the market, without losing their essence or being patronizing, and having to change their business model.

Around 70% of new entrants have to make a transition in terms of their business model. This either scares the company off completely or sees them take the "easy" path of selling to a distributor and allowing the distributor to own the brand, the business, the channels and the market. In other cases, brands who are selling B2B in China may want to add a direct to consumer (D2C) component.

Companies who are willing to add a new model and make the appropriate operational changes improve their prospects in China greatly, but it's no small feat. To enter with or transition to D2C means a brand has to develop its D2C model for the market, keep ownership of inventory, drive the marketing, develop new KPI's, take risks, and be patient.

D2C in china also means you have to invest in fully understanding who the consumers are. You have to dig deep on consumer research, data science, and cultural relevancy.

The need to be aggressive in D2C is especially urgent for consumer packaged goods (CPG) and fast-moving consumer goods (FMCG) companies who are getting squeezed out by private labeling, digital natives and challenger bands. There are a good number of companies who have made a successful transition to D2C in China and are thriving and because of it. What surprises me is the number of companies who have not yet transferred the direct to consumer expertise they've gained in China to their home or tertiary markets.

Some companies do get it though. Mondelez is a good example.

In 2012 Kraft Foods was renamed Mondelez. Mondelez boasts some of the biggest and most important CPG brands in the world including world beaters like Ritz, Oreo, Milka, Cadbury, Philadelphia, Tang, Trident and Toblerone, in addition to 65 other top brands. They're number 1 in biscuits and cookies, tied for top spot in chocolate, number 1 in candy and number 2 in gum.

They entered the Chinese the gum market in 2012 and established Mondelez China. They entered the chocolate market in 2016 with Milka. In August of 2016, the company entered into a partnership with Alibaba to develop their D2C, digital retail and New Retail business. They officially made themselves a retailer and consumer company with the launch of their Tmall store in late 2016.

Further, they made a major push across the market for the 2016 11.11 festival. At the same time the company announced that they wanted to increase their e-commerce income dramatically, and it was clear that China would play a major role in the success or failure of the initiative.

Much like Starbucks, Mondelez deftly mixed the ingredients needed for success. Know the culture, partner well, listen to the consumer, localize and be flexible. The company had lost significant market share across its major categories between 2012 and 2016 because they were late to the digital commerce/D2C play and had a lot of catching up to do. But catch up they did.

They expanded from Tmall to JD and other platforms and by the 1st half of 2018, year on year digital sales improved by 90%. Today Mondelez is a market share leader in snacks, gum and biscuits in China and their share of sales via e-commerce range between 15% and 30% of their total.

A key driver was the relaunch of Oreo and adapting the brand to Chinese tastes and ingredient preferences. They also launched a new marketing playbook that included AR-incorporating packaging and tailored packs for e-commerce and convenience stores.

They also made packaging that was more suitable for e-commerce.

Mondelez became a huge success in China. Now as the company strives to make digital and New Retail a bigger part of their global playbook, it's clear that they're incorporating what they have learned in China's New Retail landscape.

They now localize Oreo flavors, as well as the cookie's presentation and overall marketing strategies in other markets. Seeing the growth that on-demand delivery produced for their online and overall market share growth, the company joined The Loop, a service that delivers goods to homes in environmentally refillable packaging.

We are seeing Modelez start to take their experience in shifting to D2C and digital in China and making it a centerpiece of their future growth globally.

Case Study: Stadium Goods

John McPheters grew up in New York city and immersed himself in the hip hop, sports, sneaker and graffiti sub-cultures of the 1990s. After graduating college, he worked for a time at Def Jam Records in Japan and then for Nike's social media group. This was finishing school for the future streetwear meets luxury meets vintage sneaker impresario.

In 2015 McPheters and his partner Jed Stiller founded Stadium Goods. The company was conceived as an online marketplace for vintage and rare sneakers. It would be anchored at its New York City store where clients bring their sneakers, have them appraised before SG puts them up for sale online earning a commission when they sell.

Aside from taking an underground subculture mainstream and presciently seeing an opportunity for a niche digital marketplace, the company had its eyes on China from day one.

For Stadium Goods, China was not something to be considered for later expansion after the company was well established, it was a primary focus. Not long after the company started operations, it started preparing for China entry. They conducted consumer research, spoke with various marketplaces, worked out a cross border model and chose Alibaba's Tmall Global for entry.

The store opened in mid-2016. As McPheters put it, "The key moment came for us on November 11, 2016, China's Single's Day Shopping Festival. We had a big spike in sales and millions of people were exposed to our brand and business."

Stadium Goods secured $4.6 million dollars in funding from Forerunner and continued to spend significant resources on building their China business. When I caught up with McPheters in Shanghai during the 2017 11.11 Festival, he told us that sales had grown tenfold year on year since 2016. By January of 2017, the company had $115 million in sales.

Things only got bigger and better from there. LVMH, the Paris based luxury goods giants invested in Stadium Goods. "The lines are blurring. It's pretty clear that luxury customers are very, very excited about streetwear and sneakers and streetwear guys are very excited about luxury," said Stadium Goods co-founder Jed Stiller at the time. In December 2018 digital luxury retailer Farfetch bought Stadium Goods for $250 million, at that time China represented 20% of the company's revenues.

Then JD.com sold its luxury unit "Top Life" to Farfetch. Here we see a prime example of how China's New Retail market influenced the direction of three important foreign companies; Stadium Goods, Farfetch and LVMH.

In an interview with McPheters in their April 10, 2019 edition, Glossy quotes him as saying "China's a big market, and we see a lot of opportunity there. We see tons of opportunity in many markets, but that was the first one where we really planted a flag. There are a lot of lessons we can learn there that we can apply other places, but I really believe in creating content that's unique for whatever region you're servicing.

A lot of brands still repurpose content they make in the US — there's a lot of subtitle content, a lot of content that doesn't quite hit an organic resonance point with consumers. But we've done a lot, as we've expanded into new regions, to create content that's specific to the areas that we go into, and that was a big lesson for us.

The other thing is that startups, specifically, can move really aggressively internationally, because they don't have to deal with the same bureaucracy that larger, multinational organizations have to deal with. So we can see an opportunity and move really fast to try to capture it, where larger entities tend to struggle. For all entrepreneurs and startups that are trying to innovate, you can make big waves in foreign countries because of the lean nature of a startup."

Stadium Goods has continued to innovate and deploy new concepts and has successfully built the foundation for a fully realized New Retail operation.

It's hard not to notice the blend of home grown innovation and lessons learned from China's New Retail.

Brick and Mortar Matters

Stadium Goods is opening stores and has fully integrated them with their technology, logistics and marketing. In addition to their usual selection of secondary market sneakers they now sell lifestyle apparel from Nike, Adidas, Supreme, Converse, Jordan, and Asics.

Their New Retail mix includes:

- A brick-and-mortar flagship retail store in the heart of Soho

- Smart stores that tell stories and focus on experience

- Desktop and mobile e-commerce

- Order online, pick up in store

- Online scheduling for consignment appointments

- An online hub for remote consignment support

- Concierge service for VIP customers

- Integration with Farfetch, JD, Tmall and big brands

Stadium Goods was an early mover in taking a China-centric and New Retail approach to launching a business and clearly that has paid dividends for them many times over.

CHAPTER 12

Chinese Giants Going Global

When and how did China's push for widespread adoption of technology begin? In his book, AI Superpowers: China, Silicon Valley, and the New World Order, Kai-Fu Lee identifies the moment he sees as crucial.

On September 10, 2014, at the 2014 World Economic Forum's meeting in Tianjin, unnoticed by many outside China during a long speech, Premier Li Keqiang repeated the phrases mass entrepreneurship and mass innovation several times. Lee sees this as the moment the starting pistol was fired.

From then on, provincial and local officials and business leaders adopted the slogan and unleashed massive support for startup ecosystems and technological innovation. This came in the form of subsidies of all kinds. Money, space and time was given to entrepreneurs and innovators to create, work and build.

A directive from the State Council nine months later confirmed the mass entrepreneurship and innovation support and called for special zones, incubators, funding as well as favorable tax policies, low rents for businesses and streamlined business permit processes. Authorities all over China were keen to outperform each other in this new area that had been pinpointed for development and local government funding poured into tech followed soon after by venture capital.

The Central government knew that a process of shifting from manufacturing to tech-related industries had to occur and was going to occur. Rather than wait for the process to roll out over the long-term, along with all of the societal upheavals it would entail, they sped up the process monumentally.

That's the political backdrop behind China's ambitious domestic tech goals. Let's look now at how China's tech giants have not only dominated nationally but are expanding internationally.

Going Global

China as we have seen not only developed the concept of New Retail but it has a substantial lead in all aspects of bringing it to life and creating the blueprint for its globalization.

Here are some of the hallmarks of New Retail on show in modern China:

- The commitment to a unified channel merging online and offline as an operating principle and growth engine for marketplaces, brands and retailers

- The digitization of physical retail

- The use of data science, cloud computing and artificial intelligence to drive customer-centricity

- A nationwide digital transformation of business, culture and commerce

- Commitment to automation across the product, consumer, and logistics life cycles

- Social commerce that blends content, sales, CRM, services into one offering

- The near universal adoption of digital payments and the acceptance of tech companies also being affiliated with financial, investing, and banking companies

- Social media for actions and sales rather than just advertising and branding

To date, foreign brands, retailers, B2C, B2B and D2C company's main engagement with China's New Retail titans and Chinese consumers has been selling to China. Thousands of brands from around the world are selling their products in China. For them the path has been consistent with the evolution of commerce in China. They started in the early years with distribution and direct sales via physical outlets and stores. Then they added online marketplaces and retail. For others they have started and continued to sell in China via online habitats.

The biggest challenge for brands and retailers in China today is understanding that selling online or offline, or both is not enough. In order to prosper in the long-term, they must understand what New Retail is and where and how to engage the model. The main focus of the titans is still to move products and services from West to East, but the move to globalize is fully underway.

> *"New Retail is not new or revolutionary in China. Amazon started much earlier than Alibaba but on a much smaller scale. In China, they adapted the model fast and were able to execute it in a more comprehensive way as it has advantages such as low labour costs, and existing infrastructure. The implementation makes it an innovative strategy that is remodelling the retail landscape in China. Yes, I do believe it will go global but at a slower pace. New Retail will take a while for the global market to digest."*
>
> — Zachary Ang,
> Regional Business Development Manager, VIP.com

The race is on for who will win the future of retail globally. Amazon will continue to find new ways to become a player in China, and the Chinese titans will continue to explore new ways to become serious players in the US but the real battle is for the rest of the world.

There are three distinct ways in which Chinese New Retail is going global and changing the world of commerce.

1. They are globalizing their businesses and operations.

2. They are exporting New Retail models, technology and logistics globally.

3. Foreign brands and retailers are taking what they learned in China, or are observing in China and making it a part of the home market and global evolution.

Alibaba's Globalization

Alibaba has set its sights on serving 2 billion consumers and millions of businesses globally. Their stated path to attaining 2 billion users is fairly straightforward and has been consistent over the last several years.

In November 2017 and November 2018 we spoke with Michael Evans, Alibaba's Global President and Daniel Zhang, who will succeed Jack Ma as Alibaba's CEO. They laid out the company's globalization plan as follows.

China

To have 1 billion users in China through rural expansion and by enhancing New Retail services and products in developed urban areas. At the time we spoke in 2017, Alibaba had more than 400 million registered users and when we spoke in 2018 that number was more than 550 million. Today Alibaba serves more than 700 million consumers in China.

Southeast Asia

Alibaba has added 400 million consumers in Southeast Asia through its acquisition of Lazada. Lazada was an e-commerce platform introduced by Rocket Internet in 2012. It began as an e-commerce retailer, selling products directly to consumers through its warehouses. By 2014

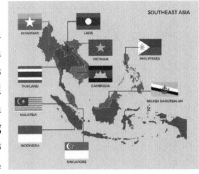

the company had expanded to include Indonesia, Malaysia, Vietnam, Philippines, Singapore and Thailand.

In 2013 the company added a marketplace model to their direct retail operations.

Alibaba acquired the company in 2014 giving it a massive head start in the region over JD, Tencent, and Amazon.

Alibaba has steadily worked to integrate all China-based Alibaba products and services into Lazada's ecosystem. It's also integrated the Cainiao logistics network with Lazada's largely owned and operated system to ensure that fast fulfilment at the regional, local and hyper-local level is achieved and three, to bring its New Retail model to the entire region.

Southeast Asia is critical to Alibaba's globalization plans. It's the 3rd largest and fastest growing digital market in the world, estimated to reach 240 billion by 2025. There are also a growing number of middle class and affluent consumers. This group made up about 40% of the total population in 2018 and is projected to reach 70% by 2030. The fast pace of urbanization is driving digital demand. On top of that, digital commerce is expected to make 6.4% of total retail by 2025 with 2/3 of that being mobile commerce.

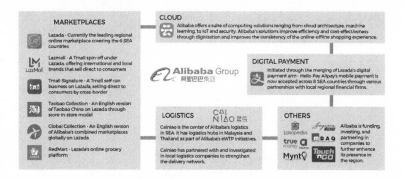

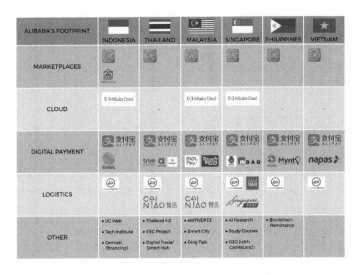

Alibaba's primary competitors in Southeast Asia are Amazon, JD.com and Tencent.

Alibaba competes with Amazon in e-commerce, cloud solutions and logistics. It leads in e-commerce through Lazada but is catching up to Amazon in cloud solutions. JD is introducing a new model in Southeast Asia that incorporates social and local services but Alibaba has a competitive advantage with e-commerce and logistics. Alibaba competes with Tencent in payments and financial services as well as cloud computing. Tencent has an advantage in social, media, entertainment and local services.

Other initiatives for Alibaba in the region include actively investing in tech unicorns and startups to expand its ecosystem in the region. Examples include:

- Zamato - An Indian-based restaurant finder and food delivery app with a presence in Singapore received $210 million USD from Alipay.

- GetLinks - A Thailand-based startup offering a job finder app in six Southeast Asian countries and neighbouring regions closed funding led by Australia's Seek Group and Alibaba's Hong Kong Entrepreneur

Fund.

- Daraz.com - A Pakistan-based online shopping platform that was acquired by Alibaba giving it access to the Myanmar e-commerce market through shop.com.mm.

ALIBABA VS. OTHER TITANS IN SEA

Alibaba is the leader in SEA market penetration with a competitive advantage above all other Titans in almost all new retail solutions.

KEY BENCHMARK	ALIBABA	AMAZON	JD	TENCENT
Commerce Offerings (e.g. type of marketplaces, country coverage, product categories coverage)				
Payment & Financial Services (e.g. payment availability, country coverage, range of product & services)				
Cloud (e.g. range of product & service offerings, infrastructure deployment)				
Logistics (e.g. delivery time, range of offerings, country coverage)				
Social, Media, and Entertainment (e.g. range of products & services, country coverage, platform coverage)				
Marketing & Data Management (e.g. product & service offerings, data quality & coverage, country coverage)				
Local Services/New Retail (e.g. offline setup, O2O, local directories, etc.)				

NOTE:

○ NONE

◔ EARLY ADOPTION

◑ ACTIVELY GROWING

◕ ADVANCED

Malaysia

Alibaba's progress is more advanced in Malaysia than in other countries in Southeast Asia. It has set up an office there with over 1,000 local hires to deepen cooperation, better serve the local needs. The office is a one stop shop for Malaysian SMEs, providing support in driving exports, offering training programs and cloud computing services.

When it opened its office, it also kicked off Malaysia Week promotions, featuring products from 50 Malaysian brands on Tmall as well as offering Chinese travelers special access to Malaysia travel and tourism products and services from 30 Malaysian tourism merchants on Fliggy.

Through Alicloud and the Malaysia City Brain project, Alibaba is deepening its partnership with the Malaysian Digital Economy Corporation. The project is aimed at reducing traffic, monitoring vehicle flows and improving urban planning across the country. The City Brain project is currently being piloted in Kuala Lumpur and will be implemented across the country in the future.

Thailand

Alibaba's planned Digital Logistics Hub in Thailand is part of Cainiao's plan to establish five hubs around the world to enable its vision of 72-hour delivery outside of China. It's been reported that it has invested $330 million USD in the hub which will be located in Thailand's Eastern Economic Coridor (EEC). It will facilitate trade among Thailand, China, Laos, Myanmar, Cambodia and Vietnam. It's expected to help Thailand sell agricultural products, provide opportunities for young people and help Thai SMEs to do global trade.

The hub will use world-class data and logistics from Alibaba and Cainiao as well as offering full-time training to local people. The logistics system will be connected with Lazada.

In May 2019, Ant Financial and the tourism authority of Thailand agreed to roll out their credit scoring program, Zhima Credit, and virtual credit card Huabei in Thailand bringing new services, privileges and special discounts for Chinese tourists. It will likely be ready to launch in September, 2019.

Indonesia and Singapore

Alibaba is entering Indonesia, the largest e-commerce market in Southeast Asia, but hasn't made significant progress due to intense competition from JD.com, Amazon, Bukulapak and others. It also faces challenges in dealing with the complexity of the archipelago and government regulations.

Singapore was the first Southeast Asian country where Alibaba established an office in 2015. The city state is a logistics hub for the company through partnerships with Singpost and Singapore Airlines.

India

Alibaba can see, as clearly as other global technology and commerce companies the potential India has as a consumer market. In many ways India appears similar to China in its early development of modern retail focused on digital commerce.

The company has opened cloud computing data centers in the market and Alicloud has partnered with Paytm, India's homegrown digital payment system. Alibaba viewed payments as a major challenge for mass adoption of e-commerce in India and "entered" through payments.

The Indian e-commerce market is projected to be worth $200 billion by 2026. Alibaba foresees a much bigger market through the lens of New Retail. That said, India is a fickle and sometimes maddening proposition for foreign brands, retailers and e-commerce players.

The issue for global brands, retailers and New Retail titans is the consistency with which India is inconsistent in its rules, regulations, and the back and forth between being a closed and open market.

Walmart bought Flipkart, India's largest e-commerce platform for $16 billion in 2018. Tencent, a Walmart partner, already had an ownership stake and a board seat. This looked like a great counterbalance to Alibaba's Lazada move. Except that less than a year later, after putting the welcome mat out for foreign retailers and e-commerce players, the Indian government drastically changed their e-commerce Foreign Direct Investment rules.

The new rules barred online marketplaces from entering into exclusive deals for selling products and having a single vendor supply more than 25% of the inventory. The rules also restrain online marketplaces from influencing prices in order to curb deep discounting.

In other words, Walmart was left with an asset that suddenly became a liability. Amazon, Alibaba and others face the same issues that hit Walmart hard.

The quest to make India the new China for e-commerce and New Retail was and perhaps still is largely shaping up to be a battle royale between Amazon, Alibaba, and Walmart. Except new protectionist laws and regulations may have altered the equation for all three companies and will likely force a rethink of India's role in Alibaba's globalization plans.

AliExpress

AliExpress, which made its debut in 2010, may be the least talked about element of BABA's globalization, yet it may be its most far-reaching. AliExpress.com is Alibaba's Englilsh language marketplace for Chinese companies, small businesses, brands, and manufacturers to sell to global consumers via cross-border e-commerce. It's Alibaba's outbound cross-border marketplace. A reverse Tmall Global if you will. It currently serves more than 200 markets around the world.

While the marketplace began with the mission of helping Chinese people and businesses sell to a global audience, AliExpress has been integrated with Alibaba's Cainiao Smart Logistics network, offers payments services and, perhaps most significantly, is a platform for companies from places other than China to sell to other countries. This is consistent with another major globalization initiative — the new and reimagined Alibaba.com.

One example is its initiatives in Spain. In March 2019, Alibaba announced that AliExpress and the Cainiao logistics solutions company had teamed up with Correos, the national postal service of Spain, to support small and medium-sized enterprises in Spain to expand and reach new global markets.

Correos said it would partner with Cainiao on designing new logistics strategies to speed up deliveries to Spain, as well as explore new ways to manage parcels in areas such as shipment classification, customs clearance, transport and last-mile delivery. Increasingly, Spanish SMEs are using the platform, as well, to reach consumers elsewhere on the Continent, as AliExpress connects consumers to merchants in 220 countries and regions in addition to China.

Alibaba.com

It's hard to believe today, but Alibab.com was the company's first, and only service for the first five years of its existence. Launched in 1999, Alibaba.com was a digital "yellow pages" for Chinese factories, manufacturers and producers, and the global companies that needed to find them.

Prior to Alibaba.com, you had two choices when seeking a Chinese producer. Get on a plane, and spend weeks traveling the country to meet with, interview and review potential suppliers, most likely attending the bi-annual Canton Fair in Guangzhou, the world's largest wholesale and manufacturing exhibit event, or hire a sourcing agent to do the work for you.

So Alibaba started as a global company as its wholesale marketplace drew interest from around the world. In recent years, Alibaba.com became something of an after-thought at the company and with global observers. It's not hard to see why. Alibaba made its name in China by launching Taobao, its C2C e-commerce platform, in 2004 and Tmall, it's brand and retail store marketplace in 2009. Taobao is still the company's biggest source of revenue and Tmall and Tmall Global opened the door to D2C e-commerce and consumer engagement to the world.

But there is a new era underway at Alibaba.com. Alibaba's corporate mission statement is not "To sell more stuff." It's "To make it easy to do business everywhere."

The new Alibaba.com is becoming a centerpiece for the mission. In 2017, after having previously invested in the company, Alibaba completed an acquisition of a New York City e-commerce and technology company called Open Sky. Led by CEO Jon Caplan, Open Sky found success in running e-commerce marketplaces, websites and flash sale campaign in the US.

After the acquisition, Open Sky was tasked with working with the Alibaba team in Hangzhou to remake Alibaba.com. So far, the effort is paying off as it's now a more dynamic and multi-functional small business tool.

Interviewed at the 2019 Consumer Electronics Show in Las Vegas, Caplan noted that Alibaba.com was at CES because it's about innovation and that the new mission is about innovation, to digitize small business, and get them online to procure and sell goods globally. He further noted that Alibaba.com is unlocking the power of small businesses to do business with others globally including sourcing, finance and logistics.

In March 2019, Alibaba also announced the launch of a co-branded online store with Home Depot. The store will feature updated and streamlined customer support, distribution and fulfillment options and it gives a huge American brand a new global sales channel through Alibaba.com.

Alibaba.com will be an increasingly important part of the company's globalization drive.

Tmall

Then in late June 2019, Tmall Global unveiled an English version of its application page for businesses. Previously, large brands were preferred and were admitted on an invitation only basis. The process was handled through Chinese language sites and communications. The new site aims to attract high quality small, medium-sized and niche brands from outside of China. As such, it also plans to add sites in Spanish, Japanese and Korean. The portal streamlines the application process and helps businesses get the most out of their presence on the platform.

The 11.11 Global Shopping Festival

As with so many things that make up part of our digital lives today, Singles' Day was invented by some bored and lonely college students at Nanjing University. In response to not having dates for Valentine's Day, they christened November 11 Singles' Day. 11.11 was chosen because it has four 1's standing in a row.

Alibaba saw the commercial potential, because a holiday's not a holiday until it's commercialized, and in 2009, they ran a Singles' Day sales promotion. Only 27 merchants signed up. Ten years later, on November 11th, 2018, Alibaba sold $30 billion USD worth of goods from 160,000+ brand and retail sellers and shipped more than 700 million parcels.

Two years ago Alibaba renamed the event the 11.11 Global Shopping Festival because it was taking the holiday global. In 2017, the event was opened up to consumers in Hong Kong and Macau and in 2018 consumers in Southeast Asia were able to participate.

Alibaba's New Retail approach features strongly during the festival. All the company's habitats and platforms interact and focus on experiences rather than just transactions and this has proven to be very successful in delivering business growth.

They launched the "11.11 Partner Plan" during 2018's Global Shopping Festival. Consumers received "energy points" when they used any app or service in Alibaba's ecosystem. This includes Taobao, Tmall, Youku (videos), Freshippo (grocery store), ele.me (food delivery), InTime (department stores), 1919 (beverage/wine and spirits stores) and more. The energy points could be redeemed for cash coupons that could be used during the Double 11 Festival.

Ele.me's New Retail orders accelerated 78% year on year during the shopping festival while user numbers grew 69%. On November 11th, the transactions at Freshippo two hours after opening exceeded the normal takings for a whole day. Sales of Remy Martin, Johnnie Walker and Hennessey grew by 200%, 700% and 125% respectively compared to their performance during Double 11, 2017.

The event is already the largest shopping event on the planet in terms of gross merchandise volume, but now the company wants it to be global in terms of its reach as well. "It will not only be a shopping festival for Chinese people, but it will attract more foreigners to participate because commerce is a borderless world," said Alibaba chief executive Daniel Zhang Yong. "We want this Chinese phenomenon to spread to the whole world."

Electronic World Trade Platform

Jack Ma is on a mission to make global trade freer and easier. To that end, he created the Electronic World Trade Platform (eWTP). According to its website, it's a "a private sector-led and multi-stakeholder initiative, for public-private dialogue to incubate eTrade rules and foster a more effective and efficient policy and business environment for cross border electronic trade (including both B2B and B2C) development."

According to a survey conducted by the WTO and OECD on small and medium-sized enterprises' access to cross-border trade, the major challenges they face include access to information about export opportunities, trade finance and logistics costs. Cross-border e-trade is proving to be a game changer for SMEs to participate in global value chains. It allows direct access to international customers and highly efficient digitalized flows of products, data and money.

Many institutions which previously focused on global trade, such as the World Trade Organization, the International Chamber of Commerce, World Customs Organization, are working to facilitate global e-commerce, but there was no forum to bring together diverse stakeholders such as regulatory entities, vendors, consumer associations, industry associations and business intermediary organizations. This enables them to assess existing regulations and best practices and advocate for rules that foster international e-commerce and trade.

The eWTP assesses the social and economic value of global e-commerce and trade in fostering SMEs, develops industry standards and rules, regulations and customs processes, consumer protection mechanisms and internet and logistics infrastructure. It also seeks to lower tariffs and harmonize taxation to facilitation of flow of goods, finance and data.

The organization also works to develop emerging markets, promote public-private dialogue to improve the business environment and cooperate with international organizations such as the World Trade Organization (WTO) in order to prioritize etrade development.

To summarize, the eWTP is Alibaba's initiative to rewrite some of the rules and provide an alternate global trade organization focused on digital commerce and cross-border commerce. It may prove to be one of the company's most effective tools in reaching two billion customers.

Alipay

Alibaba is aggressively expanding Alipay to North America, Europe and Asia. For now, it's focused on serving Chinese tourists and travelers in retail environments, but keep an eye on it. It may or may not become a widely adopted digital payment solution for everyone in the markets it serves.

China has an 80% digital payment adoption rate. Alipay and WeChat Pay are the largest digital payment systems in China and the world and almost all Chinese consumers have both on their mobile phones.

Alibaba's Europe Strategy

Alibaba is growing its teams across Europe and in London with a newly expanded staff but doesn't plan to compete toe-to-toe with local e-commerce marketplaces there just yet. The company's 2018 plans focussed on two key areas: Taking Europe to China and The Travelling Chinese.

Logistics and Alipay

The first priority for Alibaba is to connect more businesses and brands from Europe with consumers in China. Alibaba has a logistics network which helps get products from Europe to China and an advertising platform that helps build brands in China. In its latest quarterly results, Alibaba pointed to Swedish clothing giant H&M, Italian luxury fashion label Marni and Japanese sporting equipment giant Yonex as the latest luxury brands that are now selling in China via Alibaba. Alibaba's growing presence in Europe and the US is not about going after consumers or challenging Amazon or Asos.

Alibaba's second mission in Europe is to get more of its services working there for Chinese tourists. In China, mobile payments, which work by scanning a shop's QR code with a smartphone, are ubiquitous. Alibaba's Alipay, which boasts 600 million users in China, isn't accepted across most of Europe but Harrods, Selfridges and The Body Shop accept it.

AliExpress

The Polish market is dominated by Allegro but AliExpress is shaking things up. Alibaba-owned AliExpress English e-commerce site is growing fast. In the first half of 2018, the total value of its transactions was almost on par with the whole of 2017. That growth has taken place in a market that eBay tried and failed to tackle between 2008 and 2013.

Cloud Computing

The international cloud market is dominated by Amazon, Microsoft and Google while e-commerce is controlled by Amazon or local parties. Alibaba wants a piece of both markets. Central Europe, which is still a cloud frontier is a battleground of choice. On almost every list of leaders for public clouds, Amazon is in top spot with Microsoft second and Google third. The big exception to that hierarchy is in China and Asia.

Building a logistics infrastructure is not the only focus for Alibaba in Europe but building technology infrastructure is important as well.

In Poland Alibaba's cloud and attractive pricing could offer realistic options for organizations that already use Amazon Web Services. That situation makes the distribution deal that Alibaba closed last summer with Poland-based cloud services firm ABC Data relevant. Through a strategic partnership, ABC Data is now Alibaba's distributor in Poland.

In Germany, it has acquired Ververica (formerly Data Artisans), a Berlin-based analytics startup for €90 million. The company, founded in 2014, is known for its open-source platform called Apache Flink which provides data processing and streaming solutions for businesses including Dutch financial firm ING Group, Netflix and Uber. It enables the management and deployment of live data applications so they can react to data instantaneously. It can also power large-scale applications for real-time analytics, machine learning, search and content ranking and fraud detection.

Alibaba has deployed Apache Flink on a large scale and has been working with the company and supporting its open-source community since 2016. The company announced in February 2019 that it was joining forces with Alibaba to build a new initiative around open source data processing technologies.

JD's Globalization

JD, like Alibaba is rapidly expanding its reach globally with its "Internationalization" plan. And as with almost everything regarding competition with their Hangzhou based rival Alibaba, JD.com's approach to globalization differs from Alibaba's in many ways, reflecting the company's commitment to its vision of Smart Retail.

JD is one of the largest retailers and e-commerce companies in China and even surpasses Alibaba in some metrics. Their model is based on buying and owning inventory that they sell and deliver to consumers. As such they also have their own internal, state of the art logistics systems.

JD's globalization plan is based on the twin pillars of partnerships and an asset-heavy inventory and logistics model. This makes sense as JD and its partners would be unable to legitimately compete with Alibaba and Amazon globally without joining forces.

"Right now our overseas expansion efforts are focused on Southeast Asia, a market with similar characteristics to China several years ago, and where we believe the e-commerce potential is tremendous," says JD's Ella Kidron.

As another example, they have opened the JD.ID X-Mart in Jakarta. It's a partnership between JD.com's robotics and automation lab, JD-X and their Indonesian joint venture partner, JD.ID. This is the first time JD's unmanned store technology has been used overseas and the store in Jakarta offers an expanded selection including cosmetics and fashion goods, as well as standard convenience store items. This is part of their Retail as a Service strategy, and they aim to find more partners in Southeast Asia and around the world.

JD and Tencent

There may be no more important partnership in China's New Retail landscape than that of JD and Tencent. Tencent is the largest outside shareholder in JD. The companies have partnered in order to leverage their respective strengths.

JD is a giant of retailing, e-commerce and logistics. Tencent is not only a leading global technology company specializing in social media and gaming. Tencent needed a way in to the world of digital commerce and logistics and JD needed a partner that would help develop new technologies and tools and who could connect them to new consumers via Tencent's 1 billion WeChat users.

In China, the JD/Tencent partnership is the foundation for a collection of partnerships designed to build a robust retail model. Alibaba calls their version New Retail. Tencent calls their version Smart Retail and JD.com refers to their model as Boundaryless Retail. Other partners include:

- VIPshop - JD/Tencent invested $864 million in the specialty e-commerce marketplace.

- Walmart - Walmart sold their Chinese grocery unit Yihaodian to JD for 5.9% equity and then took an additional stake in 2016 and 2017 for a total of 12.1% ownership.

- Baidu - China's largest search engine

- Carrefour - French grocery giant which had its China operations bought out by Suning in June, 2019

- Google - Google invested $550 million in JD.

While these partnerships are important within China, they're really the framework for JD's internationalization.

Farfetch

Farfetch is a luxury goods marketplace founded in Europe and headquartered in London that was founded to help boutiques sell to global consumers. It has since grown exponentially as a key destination site for the luxury brands of all sizes from around the world and is now also providing e-commerce services to third-party retailers on its platform.

In 2017, JD.com invested almost $400 million USD in Farfetch. The JD partnership provided superior logistics and consumer data for Farfetch in China and Farfetch provided blueprint materials for JD's launch of Toplife, it's luxury platform. In February 2019, Farfetch and Toplife merged.

JD's 300 million users now have direct access to Farfetch's marketplace, which includes more than 1,000 luxury brands and boutiques. JD.com will leverage Farfetch's technology and logistics platforms to connect Chinese consumers. This key partnership makes JD a serious contender to become the leading global luxury marketplace that uses a New Retail approach.

Farfetch released its 2018 fourth quarter earnings in March 2019, It posted fourth-quarter revenue of $195.5 million, up 54.6 percent from a year earlier, with the number of active customers rising 31 percent over that period. Adjusted earnings before interest, taxes, debt and amortization narrowed from a $23 million loss in the fourth quarter of 2017 to a $14.6 million loss in the most recent quarter. Shares are up nearly 2 percent in after-hours trading.

JD.com invested $397 million in Farfetch in 2017, and ties between the two companies have grown steadily over the last two years, with Farfetch using JD.com's logistics network and consumer data to expand its presence in China. JD.com is one of the largest shareholders in Farfetch, which went public last year, and JD's chief executive Richard Liu sits on the marketplace's board.

The tie-up is designed to help both companies compete with larger rivals in the world's fastest-growing, and soon to be the world's largest, luxury market. Close rival Alibaba has rapidly scaled up its luxury offerings, signing dozens of Western brands to its Tmall marketplace, which has a 56.5% share of China's e-commerce sales, to JD.com's 25.8%. Late last year, Alibaba also inked a joint venture with Yoox Net-a-Porter, the largest online luxury retailer globally by revenue.

Google and Baidu

Google invested $550 million in JD.com in 2018. The investment as not just an investment in JD, but a major investment in the JD/Tencent/Walmart/Carrefour Boundaryless Retail Alliance. Google is making a major push into digital commerce. The company has been too reliant on its ad model for revenue in the past. With regulatory, privacy and challenger headwinds, the company must diversify its offerings. Google has the reach, JD has the expertise on retail and logistics. JD will likely use the Google partnership to get a back door foothold in North America, Europe and other markets.

In March 2019, JD launched Joybuy on Google Express as its first foray into D2C sales in the United States. Consumers in 48 States can buy products in 8 categories, mainly in consumer electronics, in a move that harkens back to JD's beginnings in China as the place to go for electronics online.

The bottom line is that JD and Google's partnership, and investments in many of the same companies, will allow them to challenge Amazon, Alibaba and others for global digital market share.

What Google and Baidu have in common is that as the marketplaces spend ever increasing amounts of money on pay per click ads for their products, the marketplaces grow even larger through new consumer acquisition. Eventually, as is happening now in the US with Amazon and in China with Alibaba, consumers start their shopping searches on marketplace apps and sites rather than on search engines, threatening the ad model that Google and Baidu rely on.

This is an excellent example of why a New Retail model demands companies that won't just "Stay in their Lane" and do what they've traditionally been good at. Only those who can offer brands, retailers and shoppers consumer-centricity, convenience, customization and contribution with a unified channel using uni-marketing, unified data, uni-logistics and uni-technology will make it. Google and Baidu need JD and JD needs them. Walmart needs them too and they all need each other if they're going to build an ecosystem that merges commerce, logistics, technology and entertainment.

Carrefour

It's worth noting that JD has partnered French retail giant Carrefour, which sold off its China holdings to Suning in June, 2019. JD put about 6,000 different products, including food, beverages, snacks, beauty products and 400 product categories from overseas, on its online marketplace. It's worth keeping an eye on how this partnership develops in Europe and beyond.

New Markets

JD has expanded to Indonesia (jd.id), Vietnam (tiki.vn), Thailand (jd.co.th) and Spain (joybuy.es) in the last year. The company has made Europe a priority but as we go to print it's in the midst of a reset and restructure of their Euro business and plans for expansion in France and Germany have been shelved.

South Korea

JD.com has opened an office in Seoul's central business district in an effort to connect local brands with JD's Chinese customers and to expand it's sourcing and logistics footprint in the market. South Korea's skincare and cosmetics products are immensely popular with Chinese consumers. In fact, just about anything that goes on the body or in the body made in Korea is popular including maternity and baby care items, food, drinks, vitamins and supplements. In the first half of 2018, orders for Korean products more than doubled year on year.

The 6.18 Festival

JD.com's most important festival and the centerpiece of its sales calendar is June 18th. The date marks the founding of the company. In recent years the 6.18 celebration has been adopted across all of JD's platforms and properties and by JD's competitors, much in the way that 11.11 has been adopted by Chinese brands, retailers and digital commerce players as a national festival. JD sold $19 billion worth of goods this past 11.11.

JD is drafting a plan on how to make 6.18 more international in scope but to date there is nothing substantial to speak of.

Tencent's Globalization

The 7-5-3 Strategy

Tencent is using a 7-5-3 strategy that's meant to ensure that it's not only a power in social commerce, but as a cornerstone for most aspects of B2C and B2B operations and functions and so that it's positioned for the transition to enterprise level services.

Tencent is developing 7 tools, including:

- public accounts
- mini programs
- mobile payments
- social media advertising
- security solutions
- enterprise WeChat
- new technology - big data, AI and cloud computing

It's developing five non-consumer focused offerings:

- civil services
- consumption
- manufacturing services
- health-related services
- environmental protection

And it's assuming three roles for its business partners and brands across all industry sectors:

- connector
- digital toolbox
- ecosystem builder and co-developer

We suspect that the company will solidify its positioning on 7-5-3 and then begin to roll the model out internationally. JD's Walmart, Google, Carrefour partnership is ideally set up for WeChat to becomes a more global consumer and enterprise technology and commercial services company.

WeChat

WeChat plays various roles in China's New Retail. It's a key social media site in China with a huge user base. Many users go to it for product recommendations, subscribe to brand accounts on the site, follow key opinion leaders and influencers on the site and see ads there.

At present, WeChat has a limited user base outside of China because it only offers limited functions through its international version. The technology, payments and services are all plugged into the Chinese social and business grid. Internationally, the app is a communication tool, rather than an operating system for life.

Still, at some point, we think Tencent will make a run at Facebook, WhatsApp and other local super apps in markets outside China.

WeChat's Strategy in Europe

WeChat isn't looking to replicate its Chinese business in Europe. Instead, its focus is on bringing international brands to its platform to sell more to customers in China and Chinese travelers abroad. Almost 95% of global luxury brands are on WeChat now. WeChat plans to roll out international payment services for domestic customers so Chinese tourists would have the option to use WeChat Pay in European stores.

It's also focusing on smaller European retailers with no Chinese presence. Typically, foreign companies require a Chinese business license to operate an e-commerce business but Tencent has launched a program to bypass the license if brands open up only on WeChat. Tencent brought 60 Italian companies with products ranging from furniture to food and manufacturing services to WeChat without a Chinese business license and are opening this channel to smaller companies in the UK as well.

They've also partnered with an Italian startup called Digital Retex that helps any brand integrate its services with WeChat's platform, offering a new digital shopfront.

WeChat has everything clients need to advertise in China, increase brand awareness and acquire customers in a targeted manner. WeChat manages the campaigns and does the planning so they can get traction in China.

Wechat Pay

Tencent's WeChat is an operating system for daily life for many Chinese citizens helping them with commerce, social networking, entertainment, games, appointments and payments. For many brands, it's one for the most important communication, promotions, commercial and CRM tools in China. It has more than 1 billion users and more than 800 million of them use WeChat Pay and its QR code system to pay for anything and everything, everywhere.

We've seen street musicians with WeChat Pay QR codes on their instruments and street hawkers with codes on their fruit baskets to take payments.

Tencent has engaged in an aggressive program to take WeChat Pay global. As with Alibaba's Alipay, the initial focus is on providing services to Chinese travelers, there may be foreign versions of WeChat Pay on the horizon.

E-commerce

Tencent is one of the major shareholders of the Indian e-commerce giant Flipkart, which was bought by Walmart for $16 billion in 2018. In Southeast Asia, Tencent invested in Sea Group (formerly called Garena) whose mobile e-commerce business Shopee is Alibaba's Lazada's biggest competitor. We also expect to see more Tencent involvement in the United States as the Google and JD alliance becomes more focused and active.

Gaming

Tencent is one of the largest gaming companies in the world. They've also acquired and invested in other large gaming companies. With the rise of games infused with transactions and e-commerce, this is a major position of strength for the company.

The company scored its first major hit outside of China through their investment in South Korean video game developer Bluehole Inc., creators of the enormously successful game PlayerUnknown's Battlegrounds (PUBG). Having sold over fifty million copies worldwide by June 2018 and with over 400 million total players including the mobile version, it's one of the best-selling and most-played video games of all time.

To demonstrate the potential of game-based New Retail, U.S based MAC Cosmetics partnered with Tencent in China on a lipstick promotion. As reported in Jing Daily, a digital magazine focussed on China and luxury, the pairing of makeup and a popular mobile game was as unexpected as it was successful. But MAC had done their research. They knew the game, Honor of Kings, was popular among China's Gen Z and that most of the game's players were women. In an interview with Chinese site LadyMax, MAC China marketing director Weng Yanling shared that they noticed players frequently mentioned the brand when creating lip colors for their virtual characters in the game.

MAC created five shades to match the five heroes and gained further traction with promotion from idols from popular reality show Produce 101 and other top influencers. It went viral.

The limited-edition lipsticks that were available on Tmall, MAC's website and a WeChat mini-program. Consumers placed over 14,000 pre-orders across the three platforms, and all five lipstick styles sold out across all sales channels within 24 hours of the launch. While all of the lipsticks sold out within a day, the campaign lives on in a new experiential retail space in Shanghai. Here, customers can try on lipsticks virtually and, using the brand's WeChat mini program in the store, customize eye shadow shades created by top influencers.

This is a powerful demonstration of what New Retail can be. Gaming, media, entertainment, commerce, Tmall, WeChat mini programs, technology, logistics all working together to build a brand, sell products and delight consumers.

The key pillars are all present. Customer centricity, convenience, customization/consumer contribution, a unified channel, uni-marketing, uni-technology and uni-logistics. This is the Tencent and general New Retail model we expect to go global and which we encourage you to adopt going forward.

Investments

It can be argued that more than any of Tencent's other pursuits, investment is where they are having the greatest impact on global New Retail and technology.

In February 2019, Tencent made a $150 million dollar investment in the controversial US-based message board Reddit. This event was just one in a long line of investments the company has made on a global basis over the last few years. Many people, even in the business and tech communities outside China, have never heard of Tencent. This was true even when in the spring of 2018 Tencent passed the $500 billion mark in valuation, one of less than ten companies in the world to do so.

As journalist Louise Lucas, who focusses on tech and China reported in the March 11, 2019 edition of the Financial Times, "It was just one of more than 700 investments across the world. The Chinese company has board seats on more than 400 of those companies, according to one person close to Tencent, with 30 per cent to 40 per cent of its investments outside China. Its investment portfolio is roughly twice as big as its main Chinese rival Alibaba and dwarfs those of US peers such as Facebook and Google and Tencent has no intention of slowing down, even after a record deal spree in 2018."

Tencent's goal appears to be to feed its empire, diversify, stay on top of trends and learn from co-investors like Google and Walmart while offering its investment targets the chance to access China's huge consumer base. After all, for that kind of scale, there really are only two choices, Tencent or Alibaba.

It has interests in fintech. Tencent, German insurance firm Allianz and PayPal co-founder Peter Thiel are backers of German banking app N26. As Tencent and PayPal are pioneers in mobile payments, they're great fits. Allianz, also German, is one of the most traditional finance companies in the world but it believes in making digital progress in the financial industry.

In 2019, N26 plans to process $16 billion USD (€13 billion) and wants to reach more than 5 million customers in 2020. It's planning a roll out in the US and UK soon. Some products, such as savings, investments, overdrafts and insurance are limited to Germany and Austria but they'll be offered to more markets in the future. British competitor Revolut currently processes $1.5 billion USD per month but it seems like there's enough room for both of them to grow.

True to its gaming roots, Tencent has large stakes in some international gaming companies. in 2012, Tencent acquired 40% of Epic Games. Based in North Carolina, it's famous for Fortnite, Unreal, Gears of War and Infinity Blade. It also owns 84.3% of Finnish mobile game company Supercell which makes Hay Day, Clash of Clans, Boom Beach, Clash Royale, and Brawl Stars.

In summary, Tencent is using investment, gaming, new technologies and strategic partnerships to help shape the future of retail and business not only in China, but globally.

Even if weren't familiar with Tencent, chances are you use a few of its products or the creations of the companies it owns or has invested in.

China's International Integration

The country's international ambitions have been focussed in 8 key areas.

Trade

Although this has been a highly contested arena in 2018 and 2019, China still wields enormous power in the world of trade. It became the largest trading nation in goods in 2013. It's the largest export destination for 33 countries and the largest source of imports for 65 and its share of global trade increased from 1.9 percent in 2000 to 11.4 percent in 2017. It's trade impact is higher within Asia, in sectors related to global technology supply chains and in resource areas where it serves as a large import market.

China's share of global services trade is 6.4 percent, about half that of goods trade but as of 2017, it became the world's fifth-largest exporter of services and at $227 billion in exports, it had tripled in value from 2005. It's the second largest importer of services with $468 billion in 2017, making it the second-largest services importer in the world.

Companies, Conglomerates, Investments and Acquisitions

In 2018, there were 110 firms from mainland China and Hong Kong in the Global Fortune 500 compared to America's 126. From 1995 to 1997, Chinese firms accounted for less than 1 percent of the top percentile for economic profit. From 2014 to 2016, that had risen to 10 percent. However, the average share of overseas revenue at Chinese firms stands at 20 percent compared to a global average of 44 percent and only one Chinese company is in the world's 100 most valuable brands list.

Finance

China's financial system is not globalized as there's very little foreign involvement in its banking system, bond market or stock market. There's a lot of foreign direct investment, with China being the world's second largest source of outbound FDI and the second largest recipient of inbound FDI from 2015 to 2017. However, as of 2017, its inbound and outbound capital flows were still only about 30 percent of those of the United States.

People

China is now the world's largest source of outbound students and tourists. 545,000 Chinese students studied abroad in 2017 and travelers from China made 150 million trips in 2018. Chinese students still prefer to go to the United States, Australia and the United Kingdom with students bound for these countries accounting for about 60 percent of China's overseas students. In 2017, half of the trips taken by Chinese tourists were within the Greater China area and 29 percent were within Asia. China is not a large source of or destination for migration accounting for only 2.8 percent of the world's migrant population and immigrants to China coming in at only 0.2 percent.

Technology

China's research and development spending has risen dramatically from $9 billion in 2000 to $293 billion in 2018. This makes it the second-highest research spender in the world, nearing the United States. It still relies on imports of semiconductors, optical devices, and intellectual property (IP). In 2017, China spent $29 billion on imported IP while only exporting around $5 billion. More than half of its purchases of foreign technology come from the US (31%), Japan (21%) and Germany (10%).

Data

China is home to the world's largest population of internet users, at around 800 million, but its cross-border data flows are restricted. And although China is in the top eight in the world in terms of data flows measured in bandwidth, this is still only about 20 percent of America's data flow.

Environmental impact

China is the world's largest source of carbon emissions accounting for 28% of the total. It's been investing heavily in renewable energy with $127 billion USD, or 45 percent of the world's total going toward it in 2017. As a signatory to the Paris Agreement, it reduced its carbon intensity by approximately 45% by the end of 2017 and is still seeking to reduce this further to tackle pollution issues within the nation.

Culture

China has made global cultural investment a priority. The number of Confucius Institutes around the world has gone from 298 in 2010 to 548 in 2017. It has increased its share of film financing leading to more movies being shot in China. 12 percent of the world's top 50 movies were shot at least partially in China in 2017 when in 2010, it was only about 2 percent.

In terms of global pop culture relevance and popularity, however, they fall far behind their South Korean neighbours. Their television drama exports are only about one-third of South Korea's and subscribers to the top ten Chinese musicians on a global streaming platform are only three percent those of the top ten South Korean artists.

CHAPTER 13

A Brand New Horizon

How New Retail is Changing Global Commerce

The Chinese retail market is not the only one in transition. In this chapter you'll find out more about the journey global retailers are taking into the New Retail world.

Prior to and in tandem China's New Retail changes, companies from around the world were adding their own chapters to the digital commerce revolution. They're innovating new technology, supply chains, manufacturing which are in turn powering new retail models, technologies, connections, and consumer-centric models of their own.

The big difference between China and the rest of the world in terms of New Retail is that China was the first to synthesize and integrate all of the key elements; commerce, technology, logistics, and media into massive ecosystems, while at the same time integrating digitized physical locations.

Other keys to China's 3 to 4 year lead in the reimagination of retail include:

- Chinese companies have been more aggressive in bringing their technologies and methodologies to more traditional, non-digital retailers.

- Traditional brands and retailers have acted with lightning speed to digitize and engage in New Retail.

- China's ecosystem builders, retailers and investors do not suffer from "paralysis by analysis" in the effort to smash old models and try new ones.

- They have been more aggressive and active in making investments and acquisitions in physical retail. They realized that it was just as important as the digital side of things and that physical stores were the missing key for integration.

- China has near ubiquitous digital payment adoption. Transactions totalled more than $12 trillion USD in 2018.

- Chinese brands and retailers have embraced the storytelling style of retail and technology to make it work.

These are crucial differences that explain why China has New Retail and the West is stuck in omnichannel. It's also a great opportunity to learn from what's going on in Chinese retailing.

And it's an opportunity that many still miss. This has been a consistent and puzzling reality. Brands and retailers who are killing it with new technology, uni-marketing and truly imaginative ways of doing business in China consistently fail to apply these ideas back home.

On this topic, Tanguy Laurent, Managing Partner of Creative Capital, Altavia Group, a US-Chinese retail branding agency, made some very salient points in an article posted on the JingDaily website. According to Laurent:

"Narrative-oriented brands like L'Occitane, Kiehl's, or Benefits owe their survival in China to their Chinese market development teams. Take Lancôme for instance, which sent gift boxes to KOLs [influencers] aimed at creating a unique and memorable moment. Upon reception of the gift

> *"I believe there are two opportunity flows – 'Copy to China' and 'Copy from China'. We're starting to see more of the latter, especially around mobile payments and integration with other services. For instance, for many of us based in China, it's almost unthinkable that Instagram is only just getting around to adding a shopping cart and checkout function. If they had looked at how Taobao and Tmall have integrated content, discovery, search, payments and logistics, they could have made that innovation sooner."*
>
> — Michael Norris, Research and Strategy Manager,
> AgencyChina

box, influencers were sent a private key via WeChat to open it. Inspired by the Lancôme founder's own Parisian apartment, the box was conceived as a journey through the home of the founder with an authentic piece of Paris retrieved at the end: an original postcard from the '30s or '60s with a real message written on it."

If you're still not convinced that the demands and expectations of Chinese consumers are inspiring innovation and change in the Middle Kingdom and beyond, Laurent continues:

"These days, US lifestyle industries like liquor and beauty are getting approximately 30 percent of their clientele from China, and that influences the entire retail culture of the American market. In travel retail only, strategies targeting Chinese consumers worldwide have sparked the creation of new brands all over the world. We're now witnessing a similar experience with online-to-offline retail from China to the US. This doesn't necessarily mean touchscreens and AI experiences will suddenly appear in American stores, but rather that playful design elements relating to online initiatives will be adopted."

Outside of China, the most common name for these developments is omnichannel retail. If you put "omnichannel retail" into Google's search engine, you get almost 12 million results. But when you google New Retail, you get the following results:

- New Lululemon store opening in local mall/town/mansion
- New retail locations planned for downtown mixed use development
- Retail apocalypse continues
- Retail apocalypse as 8,000 more stores to close
- Retail apocalypse
- New e-commerce growth killing retail causing retail apocalypse
- Alibaba's New Retail model, what is it?
- China New Retail potential

And several other variations on the above.

That's why we wrote this book and put the focus on New Retail. Not enough people, companies, brands and retailers know that it exists, never mind how to engage in it and how the builders of New Retail are impacting businesses in good and bad, but always big ways. Omnichannel is a stepping stone to New Retail. China is five steps ahead of the rest of the world on retail, consumption, technology and how to merge them.

Some companies are successfully employing an omnichannel model and their next step is to evolve to New Retail. Some companies are still thinking about and trying to build omnichannel as an end goal, even if it will leave them 3-4 years behind the curve. If you want to read a book about omnichannel, there are hundreds to choose from. If you want to read about and learn about New Retail, this is it amigos. The only one out.

We will round third base and bring this book home with a look at the following:

- How China's New Retail model, technologies, concepts and companies are making inroads abroad through adoption by retailers, brands, and marketplaces

- How global companies have taken what they have learned in China and brought it to their home and other markets.

- How global companies, from startups to multinationals are and are not embracing the tenets of the 4th Industrial Revolution, digital commerce and what the opportunities and consequences are.

It is worth noting here that where non-Chinese marketplaces, brands, digital retailers and others are furthest behind in New Retail is the inability to create systems that collect data at every turn. There are improvements and change is happening, but in the same way that we believe logistics deserves a seat in the C-Suite, we also believe data science should be sitting right next to it. New Retail is all about how the integration of online and offline with a data science backbone creates uni-marketing.

To wit, Alibaba collects data when someone does a search, browses, makes a customer service inquiry, makes a purchase, makes a payment, watches a video, uses and app, hails a taxi, uses Alipay, watches an Alibaba Pictures movie, takes part in an Alisports event or steps into one of their many brick and mortar properties.

Tech and E-commerce Companies

Amazon

Known as one of the world's largest online retailers, Amazon is seen as a competitor for Chinese retail giants but it's also where many Chinese-made goods are sold and where many small businesses from China do cross-border e-commerce. Its development path closely resembles that of

Alibaba Group and JD.com.

The Store of the Future - Amazon Go

Amazon Go is a new generation brick-and-mortar store where checkout is done automatically. Customers just download the free Amazon Go app before entering the store, link it to their Amazon account and scan the QR code to enter the store. Special cameras in the store's ceiling track you and the products, which have special dotted codes on them. A combination of computer vision, sensors and machine learning automatically sends signals to your virtual cart every time a product is taken from or returned to the shelves. Amazon's Just Walk Out technology charges the items automatically to your account when you leave and the items and their prices are listed in a receipt in the app.

There are currently 9 Amazon Go stores but according to a Bloomberg report, the company plans to open 3,000 by 2021.

Amazon Echo and Alexa

Amazon Echo is a smart speaker that synchronises with Amazon's voice-controlled virtual assistant Alexa. These devices have already disrupted the American retail landscape. Without typing on a keyboard or even seeing a computer screen, people can play music, do research on the internet, check the weather forecast or shop. According to a First Insight study, 53% of smart speaker owners use it to research prices and 22% say they're likely use it to research product prices in the future. A Forbes survey also found that Amazon purchases increase 29% after people get an Echo.

AmazonFresh Pickup

In order to compete with Instacart, Target, Peapod and Walmart, which has been running a grocery pickup service since 2013, AmazonFresh started its own pickup service. It requires an Amazon Prime membership and allows people to shop for their groceries online or using the Amazon app and then pick them up at the nearest store. People using the service must park their car in designated spots where store staff will bring their groceries to them once they arrive.

Amazon, Innovator, Follower, Gorilla

Amazon has been one of the great innovators, and most successful, if not the most successful companies thus far in the digital age. They have set the standards for growth and dominance in e-commerce, logistics, technology, efficiency and consumer centricity. Everywhere outside China, Amazon Prime changed the rules of fulfillment. We say outside China because customized, efficient, cheap, two day, same day and same hour delivery have been part of e-commerce in China for years.

Amazon makes their own proprietary devices, makes and sells billions of dollars worth of their own private label products, and has streaming TV, movies and music. Amazon is in ocean freight, air freight and is now building an advertising platform to challenge Google.

Jeff Bezos's greatest trick was to convince the world he built "the everything store" when what he really built was "the everything company". As Scott Wingo of ChannelAdvisor put it in 2017, there is an "Amazon-scape" made up of hundreds of commercial, technological and logistics services, entertainment products and supply chains.

Amazon's acquisition of Whole Foods, was an acknowledgement that the difference between e-commerce and New Retail was the importance physical habits had in their growth and in servicing their consumers. This mirrored Walmart's realization that the role digital commerce had to play in their future store relevance through their acquisition of Jet.com and their partnerships with key tech players globally.

Amazon was late to the realization that what consumers want most is choice. The choice to buy wherever, whenever and however they like and that even if e-commerce sales hit 25-35%, that still leaves 70-75% of purchases offline and they had no skin in that game.

Amazon's greatest achievement thus far is in being the first and only "super-ecosystem" in North America. All of the elements that make up New Retail are in place for Amazon. Their missing piece was physical, and through Whole Foods, Amazon Books, Amazon Go and most recently the experimental Amazon Pop-Ups, which have been wound down, they are on track for being a leader in New Retail in the US.

Yet, Amazon differs from its Chinese rivals in several important ways. Some in which it gains a competitive advantage and in others that may prove to be serious hindrances to its prospects in the long-term.

Data

Amazon owns the consumer data and the consumer relationship. They do not share it with the brands and retailers who sell through them. This has given them an advantage in tailoring their services, products and offerings for consumers. They have also used this data as the blueprint for creating their own private label brands which as of this writing include more than 20 categories and over 100 products. Amazon's private label sales in 2018 were over $7 billion USD and that could reach $30 billion USD by 2020. All clear advantages but it also means that Amazon is now a competitor to the very brands and retailers they depend on to sell through 1P and 3P models.

So what has Amazon learned from China's New Retail:

Physical footprints and stores matter and they must be integrated with the whole ecosystem. This is something they have not mastered yet as made obvious by the lack of vision, cohesiveness and convenience in the Amazon Whole Foods integration.

That entertainment, media and content matter. They have smartly invested heavily in streaming music, video and news.

Advertising dollars matter. Alibaba, JD and Tencent draw massive amounts of revenue from marketing, promotions and advertising in their systems. Amazon has been somewhat late to this realization as well but they are quickly catching up and ad revenue will be a major part of their revenue in the next five years.

Two Giant Companies Who are Getting New Retail Right

Walmart and Target.

Yes, you read that right.

Walmart

It would have been hard to believe as recently as two or three years ago, but brands, consumers, and partners now view Walmart as the underdog in the race to be #1 in global retail. Why? One word. Amazon. Much in the same way that Walmart once engendered a love/hate relationship with its vendors, Amazon has now become the savior/villain figure to brands.

It is no secret in the world of brands and retail that some brands love Amazon unequivocally, some don't not like Amazon and avoid them like the plague but the vast majority in the middle have a love/hate relationship with Seattle.

Consumers on the other hand have a love/love/love relationship with Amazon. The company's focus on consumer-centricity has paid off. Amazon is consistently ranked in the top 5 most loved brands in America. Sometimes trading places in the top three with Apple and Netflix.

But this has come at a cost in vendor relations. Brands love the exposure, the volume, the sales, but are becoming ever more wary as Amazon becomes their primary competitor. At numerous e-commerce and retail conferences we attended this year, there was significant buzz around the increasingly difficult situations brands find themselves in with Amazon.

Also at these conferences and in C-suites, we have consistently heard that companies are "rooting" for Walmart to get digital and New Retail right so that there is a viable alternative to Amazon.

So there it is. Walmart as the cuddly, underdog upstart taking on the biggest kid on the digital block.

Here is another one for you.

We have been bullish on Walmart for four years now. For more than three years, I (Michael) included Walmart on my list of 7 ecosystem builders that will own the next 20 years of retail.

The typical response at presentations and talks. Huh? Walmart? Didn't Amazon kill them already? Didn't they get China wrong? 2005 called, they want your "analysis" back.

For the record I also included Target in this group.

Walmart is absolutely headed in the right direction and is indeed emerging as one of the 7 key plates that will dominate retail and commerce in the next twenty years. Yes, there is still a lot of work for them to do. Yes, the JET. com buffet has not been fully digested yet. Yes, they are still incredibly asset heavy with superstores, but, they have been progressive and aggressive in developing an omnichannel first, New Retail next plan.

Walmart entered China in 1996, in the city of Shenzhen, and has grown to 424 stores in the intervening years. Since that time the company has experienced success and faced numerous challenges in the market. Initially Walmart focused on building hypermarkets in China and did what we think was a very good job of localizing the product offerings, environment and value positions.

In the end, even a thoughtful and well researched strategy for superstores and Walmart's online grocery play Yihaodian could not stand fully on their own. In addition to adding, rethinking and closing some stores, Walmart made a truly digital pivot in the market.

First, it sold Yihaodian to JD, then upped its stake in the company to 12.9%. The company is rolling out new pilot smart stores with a heavy focus on on-demand delivery. The pilot store is about 5,000 square meters, half the size of a Walmart "hypermarket,". Customers use a mini program on WeChat to shop and to check out, something they learned from Alibaba's Freshippo. The app has nearly 20 million users.

And in finally addressing on demand delivery, the partnership with Dada-JD-Daojia will enable one hour delivery within three kilometers (1.86 miles) of the store. Yes, the same size as Alibaba's "Ideal Life" delivery zone.

Walmart is also leveraging its JD-Google partnership in the US. As reported in the Motley Fool by Leo Sun:

"Walmart lacked two of Amazon's strengths: Amazon Prime, which locks in users with a growing list of perks, and Alexa, which tethers consumers to its services with voice searches. However, Walmart's new partnership with Alphabet's Google could help it counter Alexa.

Walmart recently announced that it would let shoppers buy products through Google Assistant, which runs on Google Home devices, set-top boxes, Android devices, and even iPhones. Shoppers can add products to their shopping carts by saying, "Hey Google, talk to Walmart." Could this partnership help Walmart and Google counter Alexa?

Walmart's e-commerce expansion -- which includes adding more products to its online stores, matching Amazon's prices, and acquiring a long list of digitally native brands -- boosted its US e-commerce revenue 40% in fiscal 2019. It expects that figure to rise another 35% in fiscal 2020, which started on Jan. 31."

Walmart is poised to be a major New Retail ecosystem player. It has unparalleled experience and capabilities in stores but they need to reimagine the stores for New Retail. They have one of the most robust supply chain and logistics operations in the world. They have powerful relationships with thousands of brands eager for alternative digital commerce and New Retail partners. The company has the clout, smarts and partners to leverage technology as well as a massive trove of consumer data and relationships they own. It has partnerships with Google, JD.com, Carrefour and Tencent.

Perhaps no other company in the US is better positioned to move from omnichannel to New Retail than Walmart. The blueprint was laid in China but they are adapting key elements. The only thing missing is full integration of online, offline, technology and logistics for a JD/Alibaba/Amazon like ecosystem and habitat model.

Case Studies and examples

Lowe's Holoroom

In-store VR and AR are becoming popular tools for retailers not just so customers can see what products might look like in their home but also for education and training. Lowe's, one of America's biggest home improvement retailers, developed a special Holoroom equipped with the latest VR devices for customers to learn how to paint a fence or tile a bathroom. Their studies found that the virtual reality students retained more information than a control group that watched a YouTube video. The Holoroom was developed by Lowe's Innovation Labs, which was founded in 2014 to help customers better understand home appliances and home improvement.

FedEx's Last Mile Delivery Robot

In February, 2019, FedEx revealed its last-mile delivery robot. It was designed to help retailers make same-day deliveries to their customers.

The robot was featured on The Tonight Show and can handle varying terrain as well as curbs and stairs. FedEx is working with companies such as Lowe's, Pizza Hut, Target and Walmart to assess autonomous delivery needs as about 60% of deliveries are within 3 miles.

Brands

Starbuck: From America to China and Back Again

Starbucks opened its first store in China in 1999. Twenty years later, China is second only to the United States in terms of numbers of stores and total revenue for the Seattle-based caffeine behemoth. In 2019, the company is opening a new store every 15 minutes.

Massive growth and massive profits have been mainstays of the Starbucks brand for more than 25 years. So on the surface their China growth fits the narrative, but without treating China as the unique market that it is, they could not have grown the way they have and could even have been dead on arrival. So how did they do it?

Ingredient #1 – Know Your Chinese History

When Starbucks was considering China, insiders and pundits thought the idea was crazy. "You can't sell coffee to 1 billion tea drinkers" they said. And on the surface, they were right. But what the company saw that others didn't, was the parallel between ancient Chinese tea house culture and Starbucks. Both were the "third place" between home and work. Places you could hang out, drink, eat, talk, read, work. Howard Schultz brought a modern, luxury tea house culture back to China. Then China learned to love coffee.

Ingredient #2 – Know the Your Chinese Culture

As I reported in Forbes, "From the beginning of Chinese civilization, family has been the key source of security, education and spirit for the Chinese people. The society's Confucian values entwine children and parents in a bond of shared responsibility that stretches throughout all stages of life.

Starbucks has, since 2012, hosted an annual "Partner Family Forum," where its employees (whom the company calls "partners") and their parents can learn together about the company and its future in China. In Beijing and Shanghai we had 90% participation. We did not know who or how many would come. In most cases, there were whole families. There were parents, grandparents, aunts, and uncles. It was unbelievable. It was a breakthrough for the company and a milestone for local relevancy and sensitivity."

The company has continued to build on this. In 2018 it announced the launch of the "Starbucks China Parent Care Program" which currently provides health insurance for elder parents of 10,000 employees and will likely extend to more employees.

Also, Chinese highly value their community, traditionally labeled as their "inside circles." Be it their homes, schools or companies. They turn to these circles for loyalty, information and approval of their choices.

With this in mind, Starbucks designed its retail spaces to facilitate these "circles" coming together. Unlike in the United States, where Starbucks chairs are often the quiet haunts of solitary laptop users, China's Starbucks are laid out to welcome crowds, noise and lounging. In many cases, the spaces are up to 40% bigger than in the US and have been placed in very visible and easily-accessible locations in office buildings, either on highly-trafficked first floors or mezzanine areas. The sitting areas are open format and usually have no walls -- the chairs seem to flow out into adjacent spaces, such as lobbies or walkways.

Ingredient #3 – Adopt New Retail

In China, Starbucks has added on demand delivery for 2,000+ stores, augmented reality, using the *Catch the Cat* game for 11.11 which was designed to increase sales conversions, advanced loyalty programs and they have a store on Tmall.

Most strikingly Starbucks opened a first of its kind "Virtual Store" in December 2018. As described by the company, "By transcending the traditional limitations of a single-app, to provide customers a unified one-stop Starbucks digital experience across the Starbucks app and customer-facing mobile apps within the Alibaba ecosystem, including Taobao, Tmall and Alipay. The virtual store is brought-to-life by an online management hub, developed specifically for Starbucks by Alibaba, to integrate the Company's market-leading digital experience offerings, including "Starbucks Delivers," "Say it with Starbucks" social gifting and the Starbucks® Tmall flagship store, onto one seamless and easy-to-use interface for Starbucks customers and more than 600 million mobile monthly active users on Alibaba's China retail marketplaces."

Starbucks puts convenience above all else. Mobile orders, self-serve kiosks, thousands of now digitized stores, and online branding and selling across platforms. Starbucks is ubiquitous, consumer-centric, convenient, and has made itself culturally relevant.

This next paragraph is key, and one from which all brands and retailers can learn from for their China and global offerings.

"Leveraging the transformative strategic partnership with Alibaba Group, this new milestone in the Starbucks digital strategy will significantly fuel our capabilities to provide an even more personalized and enticing one-touch digital experience for the Chinese consumer, while extending the accessibility of our digital innovations into the everyday lifestyle rituals of our customers, regardless of time or place.

Enabled by the unprecedented access to **Alibaba's ecosystem**, (emphasis ours) for one of the most dynamic and inclusive digital ecosystem in China, the virtual Starbucks **store sets a new standard in 'New Retail' experience for the Chinese consumer,"** (emphasis ours) said Xu Hong,

Vice President of Alibaba Group. "

Nike

In the past, Nike operated as a brand that worked with retailer partners and left much of the work of customer relations and promotions up to them. Now, Nike is taking full advantage of customer data and memberships to create hyperlocal digitized stores and build a new relationship with its customers.

It has apps and tech enabled shoes that provide health information to consumers. This strengthen the brand's relationship with people who use their products, provides the brand with insights about its users and transforms the brand's role to a health and fitness partner.

It's also moved to sell directly to elite customers, called sneakerheads, through its proprietary apps. These obsessed customers get first access to limited editions or new product offerings. Sneakerheads are a small source of the company's total revenue but a huge asset in terms of insight, innovation and community engagement. They are also some of the brands biggest promoters and it serves both sides well to maintain a close relationship and open communication.

Nike by Melrose, Los Angeles

In 2018, Nike opened its first live concept store in the US. It's a pilot project where tested digital and traditional approaches merge. What's unique about the store? The products on display are determined by the shopping preferences of customers in the area. Even the location was chosen by NikePlus members. Have you ever heard of a sneaker bar? Now it's a reality. Every two weeks, Nike suggests new products to keep up with the fast-changing trends in the area and experts at the bar offer 15 minute express sessions to find the right pair of sneakers for customers.

To enhance customer loyalty, Nike has installed a NikePlus Unlock Box digital vending machine, which rewards members with free products every two weeks. Another special feature is direct communication with the shop through the Swoosh Text system. The app allows customers to reserve items and pick them up at a convenient time.

Nike House of Innovation 001, Shanghai

After the huge success of Nike by Melrose, the brand continued its global expansion in Shanghai. There are art installations, workshops and products exclusive to the outlet at Nike's House of Innovation. Members of the NikePlus Club have access to Nike's expert studio, where professional athletes reveal sport secrets and designers customize select shoes in private sessions. The basement has a motion sensor digital floor where customers can trial products. Nike plans to open more innovation labs and has already opened another in New York.

Gamification - Reactland

Another recent innovation by the brand was Reactland, Nike's game concept. Nike worked with partners to develop a game that allowed customers to try their new React shoes while playing the game. Customers in shops in four major cities could play the game on site. Their pictures were snapped and an avatar resembling them was created. Players then ran while wearing the React shoes on a special treadmill in front of a green screen. Their movements and actions on the treadmill translated into movements in the game as they ran across clouds, bridges, sand dunes or rooftops in Mario style gameplay.

IKEA

IKEA Place AR Kit

In 2017 for iOS users and 2018 for Android users, the Swedish furniture company launched its IKEA Place app. With the help of augmented reality, customers can experiment and see what furniture would look like in their home. One of the most useful features is the app's accurate scaling. It automatically adjusts products to a room's dimensions with 98% accuracy. Customers just need to scan the floor of the room and select the product they want to try. Consumers can see the texture of the fabric and play with the lighting. The app also helps users to find similar pieces of furniture.

Space10 Lab

IKEA's innovation lab brings together designers, artists, engineers and others to work on sustainable solutions to future issues such as urbanization, food security, health and wellness and the explosion of new technology. Launched in Copenhagen in 2015, they've come up with concepts for 3D-printed meatballs made from alternative ingredients, such as cooked insects and leftovers, movable partitions that can easily modify workspaces and tiny home kits.

In September 2018, the lab presented Space on Wheels — its vision for the future of driverless vehicles. There were seven concepts: an office, a café, a mobile clinic, a garden, a hotel for people to sleep while they travelled, a movie theater and a pop-up shop. SPACE10 has also developed an app, which allows people to 'order' the vehicles and experience them in augmented reality.

What's Next?

The Ecosystems that have been and will continue to be built in China are the foundation for the future of commerce in China, in Asia, and globally. The "Five New" are the natural evolution of Globalization 2.0.

There is no longer a question of how much time, resources, money and people to dedicate to "online" or "offline". The word omnichannel, although still kicking around, is a dead concept and should be retired after a short and undistinguished term of service.

Every moment that companies from small and medium-sized enterprises to multi-national companies spend wavering on whether to engage China, to stick with an omnichannel game plan, hesitate to invest in digital transformation and shift away from being international to global thinking and operations is a moment that their opportunity for growth, relevance, and consumer interest is lost.

Alibaba, JD and Tencent, are all investing in the future. Tencent's portfolio of invested companies, Alibaba's acquisitions, and JD's multiple partnerships are increasing the value of their ecosystems to consumers, to the brands and retailers that engage them and the innovative technology, logistics and service companies along for the ride.

For many others they could not, or would not change and the disruption of New Retail was too fast, too hard, and too expensive.

For other brands and retailers their hubris and smugness in the face of New Retail will doom them. For others a belief that there are things that only they can do that cannot be replicated will be theirs.

The four most dangerous words in the world for the luddites and smug among brands and retailers are: Amazon can't do this. Alibaba can't do that. Walmart isn't that. JD can't do this. The digital natives can't do that.

They can, they are, they will.

Brands and retailers should not be afraid to take chances, fail fast, build their own ecosystems and engage in as many parts of the mega-ecosystems as they can.

New Retail requires you to reassess your "Four Flows" – Money, information, products and people.

Adapting to and engaging New Retail is not something that can be done all at once. It can and should be incremental. You should employ fast test and learn regimes.

New Retail requires B2B companies to think and act like B2C companies and to accelerate their D2C strategies, platforms and structure.

Far from being a time of a "retail apocalypse" New Retail, New Technology, New Manufacturing, New Finance, and New Supply Chains have created a consumer and retail Renaissance.

To finish, we'd like to provide you with some high level guidance on what you can do to engage in New Retail in China and Asia, in your home markets and on a global basis.

The Roadmap for New Retail in China and Beyond

Even after reading this book you may still be wondering why you should care about New Retail.

"I'm just a small business owner in a small town."

"My business is too big to change."

"We're #1 in our industry."

"China is not in our plans at the moment."

"We focus on stores."

"We're online only."

"We only ship containers."

"We only ship palettes."

"We're high-end luxury."

"We're mass market."

"It's too expensive."

"It's too complicated."

"We're not ready."

"It's too late."

"It's too early."

Much like the pacifist sitting on his couch who refuses to participate in the struggles, competition, and wars outside, he may find that one day a bomb falls through his roof and the war has come to him.

It's imperative that you make yourself, your brand, your retail operation, your company, your commercial enterprise, your technology, your app, your start-up, whatever size, shape or form it is in, take part in the New Retail revolution.

This book is not a how to on New Retail and digital commerce, for China or globally. There are no magic "Ten Steps to Mastering New Retail" or a "Four Secrets to The Retail Renaissance."

There is no "easy" button.

Retail is complex. Selling is complex. Making products people love is complex. Understanding your consumer's journey is complex. Understanding Chinese culture, language, history and philosophy, enough to make technology, logistics, media and commerce combined work for you is complex.

What we hope we have accomplished is having presented a cogent explanation of what New Retail is, who is driving it, who is benefitting from it, who is being challenged by it, why it was born in China, and why and how it's going global.

The digital industrial revolution, the "Five New", a democratized commercial, business and creative culture, the tools that can make anyone with talent and drive a designer, seller, producer, director, influencer, founder, retailer and world changer is here.

You must present the consumer with a unified channel that can be accessed online or offline and if you enter China, that means partnering with Alibaba, JD.com or Tencent.

But no matter where you are or where you plan to do business, no mega-legacy retailer is safe or sacred. No startup is guaranteed success. Digital-only companies are going physical. Brick and mortar companies are going digital. B2B companies need to add and bulk up on D2C. D2C companies are finding new routes to profit in B2B. Retailers are brands. Brands are retailers and everyone and everything is a private label.

That's why we hope you care. No matter who you are, where you are, what you are or who you want to be as a person, brand or organization.

Things. Have. Gotten. Real.

No matter what happens with the current trade standoff between China and the US, retailers who bury their heads in the sand do so only to their own detriment. The next retail revolution is here.

Don't miss out.

ACKNOWLEDGEMENTS

This book has been a team effort and we're grateful to the many people who have helped us make it a reality. First and foremost a big thank you goes to the wonderful Alarice team that contributed writing, research, design and their many talents: Mason Ku, Natalia Drachuk, Jackie Chan, Dawn Dong, Xingqi Xu, Elaine Zhang, Eric Tse, Jacqueline Chan and Ericson Bernardo.

To our fantastic editor Maureen Lea, who made the book flow. :)

With special thanks to:

Michael Norris

Carson McKelvey

Ella Kidron

Anson Bailey

Reza Nobar

Zachary Ang

ABOUT THE AUTHORS

Ashley Dudarenok is a serial entrepreneur, professional speaker, vlogger, podcaster, media contributor and female entrepreneurship spokesperson. Her trademark expression is "Let's go get them," and she does. She's fluent in Mandarin, Russian, German and English. As a marketer and social media agency head with more than twelve years of professional experience in China and Hong Kong, she's seen the transformation of China's online world firsthand. Her specialties are China market entry, Chinese consumers, social media and New Retail.

Ashley is the founder of multiple companies, including social media marketing agency Alarice and training enterprise ChoZan. Through Alarice, she and her team help clients from overseas make a splash on Chinese social media and help Chinese brands conquer western social media. Through ChoZan, which specializes in social media education and training, Ashley does corporate trainings, executive masterclasses and speaking engagements.

Ashley frequently appears in Forbes, CNBC, the Huffington Post, the SCMP, TEDx and more. She's the host of the AshleyTalks Podcast, where she interviews top thought leaders from across Asia about entrepreneurship, China and tech.

Ashley loves to travel with her husband, box, play tennis and swim. She's fond of Shakespeare, live theater and watercolor painting.

Connect with Ashley on:
Linkedin.com/in/AshleyGalina
YouTube.com/c/AshleyTalksChina
Instagram.com/Ashley.Lina
Facebook.com/AshleyTalksChina
Twitter.com/AshleyDudarenok

Learn more at: _ashleytalks.com_, _chozan.co_ or _alarice.com.hk_
Listen to the AshleyTalks podcast: _www.ashleytalks.com/podcasts/_
For speaking engagements or marketing training: contact Ashley's team at _ashley@chozan.co_

Michael Zakkour is a digital commerce evangelist, retail futurist and vice president of the Asia Market Strategy and Global New Retail Strategy practices at consulting firm Tompkins International. He and his team provide strategic counsel for clients across a wide range of categories and industries. Michael's unique career journey, which includes e-commerce, technology, Web 1.0 and 2.0, 17 years in China consumer, market, retail, supply chains and logistics, has positioned him to guide brands, retailers and companies of all kinds to succeed in Asia and beyond as the digital industrial revolution unfolds.

He is the co-author of the 2014 Wiley best seller China's Super Consumers: What 1 Billion Customers Want and How to Sell it to Them and writes extensively about digital commerce, retail, branding, China/ APAC business, New Retail, consumers and technology. He is frequently featured on global media platforms for his expertise and opinions including the BBC, NPR, USA Today, The Wall Street Journal, Forbes, Jing Daily, NBC News, Fox Business and others. Michael is also a sought after keynote speaker and has entertained and informed audiences around the world with his electric storytelling style presentations. He is a passionate Arsenal Football Club supporter, antiquities collector and amateur historian who eats, flies and talks frequently.

Connect with Michael on:

Linkedin - *https://www.linkedin.com/in/michael-zakkour*

Twitter - *@michaelzakkour*

BIBLIOGRAPHY

1. Lee, Kai-Fu. (2018). AI Superpowers: China, Silicon Valley, and the New World Order. United States: Houghton Mifflin Harcourt.

2. Nunlist, Tom (Ed.). (2018). China's Evolving Consumers: 8 Intimate Portraits. Hong Kong: Earnshaw Books. (Contributors: Tom Nunlist, Ashok Sethi, Sacha Cody, Zoe Hatten, Annie Fang, Elisabeth de Gramont, Sizhang Kong, Francesca Hansstein, Francis Baaolino, Forrest Cranmer)

3. South China Morning Post. Perez, Bien (October 13, 2016). E-commerce will become a 'traditional' business, says Alibaba's Jack Ma. Retrieved May 7, 2019, from *https://www.scmp.com/tech/china-tech/article/2027744/e-commerce-will-become-traditional-business-says-alibabas-jack-ma*

4. McKinsey Global Institute. (July, 2019). China and the world: Inside the dynamics of a changing relationship. Retrieved July 9, 2019, from *https://www.mckinsey.com/~/media/mckinsey/featured%20insights/china/china%20and%20the%20world inside%20the%20dynamics%20of%20a%20changing%20relationship/mgi-china-and-the-world-full-report-june-2019-vf.ashx*

5. CNBC. Brown, Ryan. (October 3, 2018). Tencent-backed mobile bank N26 launches in the UK and plans US expansion by early 2019. Retrieved July 8, 2019, from *https://www.cnbc.com/2018/10/04/tencent-backed-german-fintech-bank-n26-launches-in-the-uk.html*

6. South China Morning Post. Dai, Sarah (June 26, 2019). Alibaba ramps up global e-commerce expansion with launch of English Tmall portal. Retrieved July 4, 2019, from *https://www.scmp.com/tech/e-commerce/article/3016170/alibaba-ramps-global-e-commerce-expansion-launch-english-tmall*

7. Quartz. Horwitz, Josh (June 19, 2018). There's an unexpected alliance between Google and two Chinese tech giants. Retrieved May 15, 2019, from *https://qz.com/1308872/google-forms-unexpected-alliance-with-chinas-tencent-jd-com/*

8. Alizila. Brennan,Tom (June 19, 2017). Alibaba's New 'Uni Marketing' a Game Changer for Brands. Retrieved May 13, 2019, from *https://www.alizila.com/alibabas-new-uni-marketing-game-changer-brands/*

9. Sheykin, Henry (November 12, 2018). The Game of E-com Giants: Amazon vs Walmart vs Alibaba. Retrieved June 20, 2019, from *https://medium.com/swlh/the-*

game-of-e-com-giants-amazon-vs-walmart-vs-alibaba-2fe21e92ed99

10.   Lee, Kai-Fu (November 30, 2017). Kai-Fu Lee on the merging of online and offline worlds. Retrieved May 14, 2019, from *https://medium.com/@kaifulee/kai-fu-lee-on-the-merging-of-online-and-offline-worlds-a590efd37d75*

11.   South China Morning Post. Rapp, Jessica. (March 25, 2018). Why Western fashion brands fail in China, and tips on succeeding in a country where millennial consumers are taking over. Retrieved June 12, 2019, from *https://www.scmp.com/lifestyle/fashion-beauty/article/2138570/why-western-fashion-brands-fail-china-and-tips-succeeding*

12.   Consultancy UK. (August 3, 2017). Chinese consumer market set to grow by $1.8 trillion by 2021. Retrieved April 20, 2019, from *https://www.consultancy.uk/news/13787/chinese-consumer-market-set-to-grow-by-18-trillion-by-2021*

13.   Nike. (October 03, 2018). Five Facts to Know About Nike's New House of Innovation in Shanghai. Retrieved March 11, 2019, from *https://news.nike.com/news/five-facts-to-know-about-nike-s-new-house-of-innovation-in-shanghai*

14.   Ali Research and Bain and Company. (By Jason Ding, Bruno Lannes, Larry Zhu, Hongbing Gao, Liqi Peng, Fei Song and Zhengwei Jiang) (March 13, 2019). Embracing China's New Retail. Retrieved June 24, 2019, from *https://www.bain.com/insights/embracing-chinas-new-retail/*

15.   Smart Cities World. (March 5, 2019). UN-Habitat in Chinese partnership to use AI to create smarter cities. Retrieved May 21, 2019, from *https://www.smartcitiesworld.net/news/news/un-habitat-in-chinese-partnership-to-use-ai-to-create-smarter-cities-3919*

16.   Graham, Peter. (May 21, 2019). China's VR Star Theme Park is a Vision of the Future, But not for Western Audiences. Retrieved June 10, 2019, from *https://www.vrfocus.com/2019/02/chinas-vr-star-theme-park-is-a-vision-of-the-future-but-not-for-western-audiences/*

17.   Okame, Kosuke (May 4, 2017). China's revolutionary O2O supermarket chain. Retrieved June 18, 2019, from *https://asia.nikkei.com/Business/China-s-revolutionary-O2O-supermarket-chain*

18.   Sheehan,Alexandra (February 21, 2018). How These Retailers Use Augmented Reality to Enhance the Customer Experience. Retrieved May 12, 2019, from *https://www.shopify.com/retail/how-these-retailers-are-using-augmented-reality-to-enhance-the-customer-experience*

19.   Saiidi, Uptin. Pan, Y. (January 24, 2019). China will this year surpass the US in total retail sales for the first time: Forecast. Retrieved March 6, 2019, from *https://www.cnbc.com/2019/01/24/china-to-surpass-the-us-in-retail-sales-for-the-first-time-*

forecast.html

20. Rogers, Charlotte. (July 26, 2018). Alibaba's CMO on why marketers cannot 'lag behind reality'. Retrieved January 6, 2019, from *https://www.marketingweek.com/alibaba-marketers-cannot-lag-behind-reality/*

21. Cheung, Man-Chung. (December 5, 2018). China Retail and Ecommerce 2018: The Convergence of Online, Offline and Technology. Retrieved June 16, 2019, from *https://www.emarketer.com/content/china-retail-and-ecommerce-2018*

22. South China Morning Post, Soo, Zen. (September 18, 2018). Alibaba says New Retail strategy is paying off as Hema shopper data shows bigger average spending. Retrieved May 9, 2019, from *https://www.scmp.com/tech/enterprises/article/2164651/alibaba-says-new-retail-strategy-paying-hema-shopper-data-shows*

23. Long, Danielle. (September 3, 2018). JD.com partners with hotel brands to push 'boundaryless retail' strategy. Retrieved June 7, 2019, from *https://www.thedrum.com/news/2018/09/03/jdcom-partners-with-hotel-brands-push-boundaryless-retail-strategy*

24. Forbes. Walton, Chris. (August 8, 2018). Alibaba's New Retail Could Be What Makes American Retail Great Again. Retrieved April 27, 2019, from *https://www.forbes.com/sites/christopherwalton/2018/08/08/alibabas-new-retail-could-be-what-makes-american-retail-great-again/#18ff78106079*

25. Open Gov. Bhunia, Priyankar. (February 1, 2019).China's first smart hospital featuring AI opened in Guangzhou. Retrieved June 20, 2019, from *https://www.opengovasia.com/chinas-first-smart-hospital-featuring-ai-opened-in-guangzhou/*

26. Bloomberg News, (With assistance by Heng Xie, and Yinan Zhao. (July 9, 2019) Facebook's Libra Must Be Under Central Bank Oversight, PBOC Says. Retrieved July 9, 2019, from *https://www.bloomberg.com/news/articles/2019-07-08/pboc-says-facebook-s-libra-must-be-under-central-bank-oversight*

27. Hawkins, Andrew J. (March 13, 2018). Waymo's fully driverless minivans are already putting people to sleep. Retrieved July 8, 2019, from *https://www.theverge.com/2018/3/13/17114194/waymo-driverless-minivan-arizona-early-rider-video*

First printing, 2019
ISBN 978-0-692-04191-8
10F, Iuki Tower,
5 O'Brien Road,
Wan Chai
Hong Kong